Group Care

with Children

and

Young People

Second edition

Neil Thompson

Russell House Publishing

First edition published in 1998 by:
Prospects Publishing, Wrexham.

Second edition published in 2004 by:
Russell House Publishing Ltd.
4 St. George's House
Uplyme Road
Lyme Regis
Dorset DT7 3LS

Tel: 01297–443948
Fax: 01297–442722
e-mail: help@russellhouse.co.uk
www.russellhouse.co.uk

British Library Cataloguing-in-publication Data:
A catalogue record for this book is available from the British Library.

ISBN: 1-903855-41-1

Typeset by Saxon Graphics Ltd, Derby
Printed by Cromwell Press, Trowbridge

About Russell House Publishing

RHP is a group of social work, probation, education and youth and community work practitioners and academics working in collaboration with a professional publishing team.

Our aim is to work closely with the field to produce innovative and valuable materials to help managers, trainers, practitioners and students.

We are keen to receive feedback on publications and new ideas for future projects.

For details of our other publications please visit our website or ask us for a catalogue. Contact details are on this page.

For Helen and David

Contents

Foreword

This timely new edition of *Group Care with Children and Young People* will be very widely welcomed because it provides authoritative guidance for everyone who is involved in this field, whether directly or indirectly, on the most important problems that they may face.

The need for specialised training of those responsible, at every level, for the care of looked after children has been recognised increasingly in recent years and Professor Neil Thompson's book is likely to be regarded as an essential primer for this purpose. In successive chapters he deals clearly and thoroughly with the broad spectrum of problems underlying the complaints that were heard, for example, in the evidence before the recent North Wales tribunal. These problems range from the initial assessment of children's needs, through care planning (including the preparation of young people for discharge from care) to the daily issues that may arise in dealing with them in stressful situations.

In the latter context I commend particularly Chapters 5, 6 and 7 of this book, in which Professor Thompson tackles the most difficult matters with which a care worker may have to deal. Thus, whenever abuse, in whatever form, is alleged or suspected, a highly sensitive approach to the complainant or victim will be necessary if full and frank information is to be obtained; and equal sensitivity thereafter is required if remedial action is to be effective and in the best interests of the child. Again, physical intervention to restrain a misbehaving and often highly stressed child is an acute and recurring problem on which there has been little authoritative guidance in the past but here Professor Thompson sets out a principled approach, which will be of great practical assistance to those who have to make quick decisions on the spot when violence is threatened or occurs.

Finally, may I endorse warmly what Professor Thompson has to say in his concluding chapter about the 'learning cycle'. The need for continuous professional development cannot be over-emphasised and this book should be regarded as an ever-present resource in the development of individual carers' skills.

Sir Ronald Waterhouse, GBE, LLD

Preface

This book has been designed to help you learn about your job in group care with children and young people by exploring many of the issues that arise in dealing with children when they are living away from home or in the care of others during the day – for example, at family centres. It is to be hoped that you will find it interesting, stimulating and thought provoking, as well as practical and of direct use to you in your day-to-day work.

It is important to clarify what is meant by 'group care'. Many people seem to regard it as referring to work undertaken in children's homes. However, the term is in fact broader than this, as it incorporates work in family centres (residential or otherwise), hospitals, residential schools and other such settings. Such work is difficult and demanding, but it is also rewarding.

People outside of this sphere of work often do not appreciate what is involved and do not understand how much of a challenge it can be, nor what rewards it can bring at times.

The 'Introduction' explains the contents of the book and how you should use it to gain maximum benefit from the time and energy you devote to your own training and development.

You are an important part of the service provided for children in need and their families. I hope this book will help to equip you to do your job successfully and to cope with its many pressures.

Although the book can be used as an independent learning resource in its own right, you are likely to find it useful to use the book in conjunction with two others. *Understanding Social Care: A Guide to the Underpinning Knowledge Requirements for the S/NVQ Awards in Care at Level 4* by Neil Thompson and Sue Thompson (Russell House Publishing, 2002), although not specifically geared towards group care with children and young people, contains a lot of relevant material in relation to social care more broadly. *People Skills* by Neil Thompson (2nd edn, Palgrave Macmillan, 2002) is broader still, addressing the skills required to undertake a wide range of roles in what can be called 'people work'. However, the issues covered in that book are also very relevant to group care with children and young people. It is by no means essential that you use this book in conjunction with the two recommended here but you are likely to find it very helpful if you do.

Learning is usually an enjoyable and exciting process. I particularly hope that this book will play a part in ensuring you enjoy developing the skills and knowledge you need. There are exercises in each of the eight chapters. These are geared towards helping you understand the ideas presented and to link them to your own practice experience. I recommend that you use a notebook or pad of paper to record your notes in response to these exercises. If you are pursuing an NVQ or SVQ qualification, you may find it helpful to use these notes as part of your portfolio. This is something you should talk to your mentor or assessor about.

The Author

Neil Thompson is an established educator, consultant and author in the fields of social welfare and of human relations more broadly, with a national and international reputation. He is the author of numerous books and articles and regularly acts as an advisor to major international publishers. Neil is a Fellow of the Chartered Institute of Personnel and Development, the Institute of Training and Occupational Learning and the Royal Society of Arts and a member of the British Psychological Society. He holds qualifications in social work; training and development; mediation and alternative dispute resolution; and management, and has extensive experience in social work and related fields.

Neil was formerly Professor of Applied Social Studies at Staffordshire University. He is now the Managing Director of Avenue Consulting Ltd and Learning Curve Publishing (www.avenueconsulting.co.uk). He has been a speaker at seminars and conferences in the UK, Greece, Norway, the Netherlands, Australia, Canada and the United States. He is the editor of *The British Journal of Occupational Learning* (www.traininginstitute.co.uk) and was responsible for setting up the self-help website, www.humansolutions.org.uk. His books include:

Stress Matters, Pepar Publication, 1999.
Understanding Social Work: Preparing for Practice, Palgrave Macmillan, 2000.
Anti-Discriminatory Practice, 3rd edn, Palgrave Macmillan, 2001.
People Skills, 2nd edn, Palgrave Macmillan, 2002.
Understanding Social Care: A Guide to the Underpinning Knowledge Requirements for the S/NVQ Awards in Care at Level 4, (with Sue Thompson) Russell House Publishing, 2002.
Loss and Grief: A Guide for Human Services Practitioners, (editor) Palgrave Macmillan, 2002.
Building the Future: Social Work with Children, Young People and their Families, Russell House Publishing, 2002.
Communication and Language: A Handbook of Theory and Practice, Palgrave Macmillan, 2003.

Acknowledgements

I am very grateful indeed to Sir Ronald Waterhouse for kindly providing the Foreword. I am also grateful to Geoffrey Mann of Russell House for the important role he has played in bringing about this second edition. Duncan Pritchard of Aran Hall School also deserves thanks for his helpful comments on the chapters relating to disability and challenging behaviour and on the typescript as a whole.

Susan Thompson, as always, has been an essential part of the process of making the book a reality. I remain very much indebted to her and very appreciative of her contribution to all that I do.

This book is based on materials originally produced on behalf of Clwyd Social Services Department and subsequently published by Prospects Publications. The publishers are grateful for their permission to make this work available to a wider readership.

Introduction

This book attempts to provide you with a significant proportion of the basic knowledge you need to do your job effectively. The key concepts and issues relating to group care are clearly explained and are illustrated with relevant practice examples, helpful diagrams and so on. Guidance on good practice is given, including advice on how to avoid some of the common pitfalls and how to develop the skills which make for good child care.

But it is not simply a matter of reading and learning in a passive way. At certain points in the text you will be asked to do an exercise geared towards helping you put the ideas into action, to link theory to practice. Some of these exercises will ask you to think of examples from your own work to help make the ideas presented more concrete and more closely related to real-life situations. At times you will be asked to discuss issues with your colleagues and this will help you to broaden your views. You can learn from each other's experience and this will also help you feel part of a group learning together, rather than simply an individual following an isolated course of study.

In each of the eight chapters you will find a section entitled 'Guide to further learning'. These sections will provide a list of recommended books, articles or other reading material that we feel will help you to develop your knowledge and skills in the area of work concerned, as well as details of relevant websites. There will also be a range of suggestions for a variety of other ways in which your future learning can be enhanced and consolidated.

What does the book cover?

The book is divided into eight chapters. Chapter 1 provides an overview of the developments in law and social policy which have combined to produce the current framework of group care with children and young people. It is this framework or context which sets the expectations for modern social care practice. By developing an understanding of these issues, you will be helped to make sense of the foundations on which your work is built.

In addition, Chapter 1 also addresses the question of equality. It explains why good child care practice must be anti-discriminatory practice. It explores how issues of class, gender, race and culture play an important part in child development in particular and child care in general.

Chapter 2 moves on to look at children's needs. This includes the various aspects of child development, as well as a consideration of how children and young people can be helped to cope with stress, change, rejection, loss and grief. This chapter also looks at how the behaviour and attitudes of children and young people can owe a great deal to the pressures which arise when these needs are not met.

Chapter 3 focuses on care planning and the various processes involved in developing clear and realistic plans. Developing individual care plans is a basic foundation of good practice. This chapter therefore examines the role of assessment and outlines what is required to complete this vitally important task. A key theme of this chapter is that of partnership. This is partly in recognition of its key role in the Children Act 1989 and partly because it is an essential part of good child care.

Chapter 4 is devoted to the development of communication skills. Good practice in group care with children and young people requires effective communication with both children and adults. This section therefore covers three main areas. The first to be tackled is the area of verbal skills, including how to get your message across and how to ensure you are listening effectively to the messages others are trying to give to you. The second of the three areas is the use of written communication. This includes report writing and other tasks where it is important that you write clearly, succinctly and accurately. The third area is that of body language. Sometimes our facial expressions or other aspects of non-verbal communication can be extremely expressive. It is therefore important to recognise what 'signals' our body language transmits to others and what their body language is saying to us.

Chapter 5 concentrates on issues of child abuse. It covers the basics of what you need to know in terms of child protection procedures – the official guidelines on what you should do if you suspect abuse has taken place or is taking place. In addition, guidance is given on how to recognise possible indicators of abuse and how to deal with disclosures of abuse from the children or young people in your care. This chapter also explores possible ways of helping children and young people cope with the aftermath of abuse and the traumatic effects this can have on their thoughts, feelings and behaviour. Finally, in this chapter, we also consider the effects dealing with child abuse can have on us as workers.

Chapter 6 explores issues relating to disability, covering both physical and learning disabilities. It discusses some of the common forms of disability, their implications for the children and young people concerned and for those caring for them. This chapter also challenges some of the common myths surrounding disability and warns of the dangers of adopting an unduly negative approach to disability and disabled people (building on the discussion of values in Chapter 1).

Chapter 7 is concerned with an aspect of practice that many staff understandably find difficult, namely dealing with challenging behaviour. It discusses how aggression and other forms of difficult behaviour can be prevented and how they can be managed if attempts at prevention fail. The issues covered are complex ones, and there is no guarantee that any approach to challenging behaviour will be effective. However, there is much that we can do to minimise the chances of problems arising and to maximise the chances of our attempts to handle difficult situations being successful.

Chapter 8 is the final chapter, and has as its topic the various skills involved in 'self-management': this involves looking at how we are best able to function as child care workers by maximising our personal effectiveness. This includes dealing with conflict, managing pressure and stress and making the best use of the time available to us through time management techniques.

Following Chapter 8 there is a relatively brief concluding section which summarises the main points raised and offers some pointers for future learning to consolidate, and build upon, the foundations laid by studying this book.

Integrating theory and practice

It is to be hoped that you will feel able to 'integrate theory and practice' – that is, to be able to draw on the professional knowledge base discussed here and to use its insights to inform practice. There are a number of stages you will need to go through if you are going to be able to achieve this. You will need to go through what has become known as the 'Learning Cycle' (see Kolb, 1984). This involves the following steps:

1. Experience

This covers both our general day-to-day experience and specific learning experience (reading an article or book, attending a course). This experience is the basis of our learning;

it provides the foundation stones for professional development. In other words, doing is a central part of learning.

2. Reflection

But 'doing' is not enough on its own. We don't automatically learn simply through having experiences, no matter how valuable they might be as learning opportunities. Before learning can take place we need to reflect upon our experiences. We need to think about them and consider their significance.

3. Conceptualisation

Thinking about our experience won't get us very far unless we are able to relate it to other ideas and experiences or our previous learning in general. In short, we need to start to form an overview, to make connections by linking together the various aspects of our patterns of thoughts, feelings and experiences. We must begin to form our own 'mini-theory' or framework of ideas.

4. Experimentation

To complete the cycle of learning we must try out our mini-theory and we must test it by putting theory into practice. By doing this, we make our learning concrete and real, and this is the type of learning which can improve practice and help us provide a better service.

The process of learning is a cyclical one. As we reach Stage 4 we begin the cycle once again as the experimentation of Stage 4 becomes the learning experience of Stage 1 (see Figure 1). Don't worry if this process of learning isn't entirely clear to you yet. We will come back to it later in the book. For the time being it is important to remember that, as you read through the book, you will need to bear in mind that it is necessary for you to:

(a) Reflect upon what you read; think about the issues raised;
(b) Start to form links between what you read here and what you already know from your previous learning; start to piece it all together, as far as you can;
(c) Start to put your learning into practice; identify ways in which the ideas can help you do your job.

(For a worked example of the learning cycle being used see Thompson *et al.*, 1994, Chapter 1).

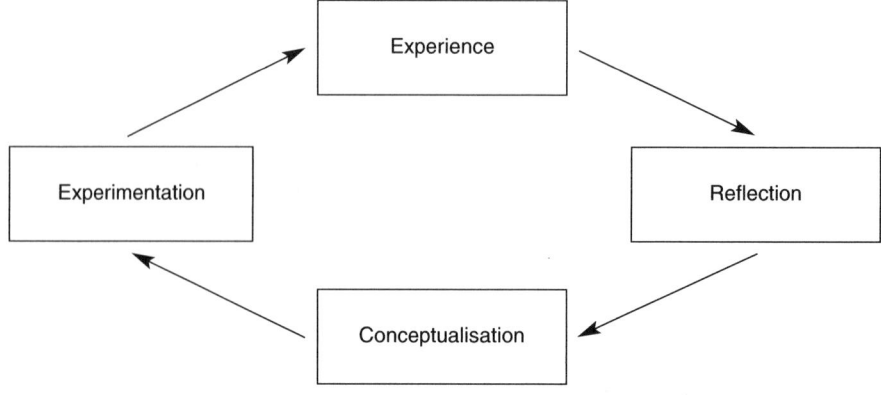

Figure 1   Kolb's learning cycle

It is also as well to remember that learning should not be a 'solo' venture and you should be encouraged to share your thinking with colleagues, friends or anyone else you can persuade to listen to you! Sharing ideas with others not only helps you to widen your perspective and learn from their experience, it also helps to develop confidence – especially when it gets to the tricky bit of putting the ideas into practice.

Getting started

We are now ready to draw the preliminaries to a close and make a start on getting down to the main business. Group care with children and young people is a difficult and demanding job which takes skill, patience and courage. This book cannot give you all the answers, but it can help you to tackle this job by offering you:

- summaries of key concepts and issues;
- practical advice and guidance;
- suggestions for further learning and development;
- the opportunity to share your ideas and learning with others and be able to use them as a learning resource too;
- a contribution to the motivation you need to carry on learning and developing.

It is to be hoped that you will find the book helpful, and I particularly hope that both you and the children and young people you care for will benefit from what the book has to offer.

Context and Values

Introduction

This chapter focuses on the context in which child care practice takes place. This is not simply a matter of setting the scene for the remaining seven chapters, but rather a very important part of understanding the basic aims, policies and values which govern group care with children and young people. In short, it is the context which 'sets the expectations'. To understand fully the expectations upon you in terms of what your job entails and how you should go about it, it is therefore necessary for you to have at least a basic understanding of the underlying context of your work.

This context can be divided up into two main parts. First of all, we shall look at the historical background, albeit in broad outline only, and note the key factors which have led to the current system of child care. Second, we shall consider the value base which underpins group care practice. In particular, we shall focus on the values of equality and anti-discrimination. We shall explore the underlying reasons for the basic principle that good child care practice must be anti-discriminatory practice. In tackling these issues, we shall see why such issues as class, gender, race and culture play such an important role in child care.

It is therefore hoped that, by the end of Chapter 1, you will have a clear picture of the broad historical developments that have produced the modern context of your work, as well as the values that are helping to shape its current and future forms.

The historical context

The care of children away from their families has a long history. For example, the church has been involved in providing care for orphans since the Middle Ages, although the nature, quality and extent of care offered varied considerably.

In the eighteenth century, philanthropists such as Thomas Coram became concerned enough about the plight of so many children to set up facilities for their care, although these again were very limited in their scope and effectiveness. It was only with the introduction of the Poor Law Amendment Act 1834 that the state recognised in the form of law, that children had a right to minimum standards of care. However, these standards were extremely basic, and many died in the squalid conditions in workhouses.

Significant changes in the plight of destitute children only began to take place in the Victorian period largely, but not entirely, due to the stronger emergence of philanthropy at that time. In particular, the influence of one philanthropist, Dr John Barnardo, stands out as a major contributor to a more humane and caring approach to the care of children who, for whatever reason, could not be cared for by their own parents. Dr Barnardo played a very active and significant part in helping children in need, but his impact and influence go far beyond his own lifetime. The Barnardo's organisation continues to provide much needed services to this day, although the emphasis is now much less on residential care and more on preventative and community support services.

Dr Barnardo had been perturbed to find how many children were homeless and sleeping on the streets of London. In response to this he set up a home for such children to ensure that they had at least basic accommodation. This home for boys was established in East London in 1870 and a home for girls was founded in 1876. Before his death in 1905 Dr Barnardo had set up more than ninety such homes and had thus established himself as a pioneer in the care of destitute children. However, it is not simply the setting up of these homes that proved so influential, it was also the development of the philosophy on which they were run.

Dr Barnardo went against much of the dominant thinking of his time by seeing children's behaviour and personality as being determined by how they were brought up rather than by fixed or inherited characteristics. Today his views may seem simple and obvious but, in his time, this was quite a radical departure from what was accepted as 'common sense' thinking. Dr Barnardo's philosophy was one of hope, as it meant that there was scope for overcoming the negative effects of the squalor, loss and rejection to which the children had been subject. He saw the possibility of working with deprived children to help them better themselves, to become law-abiding citizens with self-respect and a constructive part to play in society. This philosophy has now underpinned residential child care practice for over 130 years. Although Dr Barnardo's work has proved so influential, residential work with children in the form that we know it today began to take shape in the 1940s as part of the development of the Welfare State.

Descriptions of the birth of the Welfare State usually refer to the Three Pillars of the Welfare State: the National Health Service, Social Security and related benefits (National Assistance as it was originally called) and compulsory secondary education.

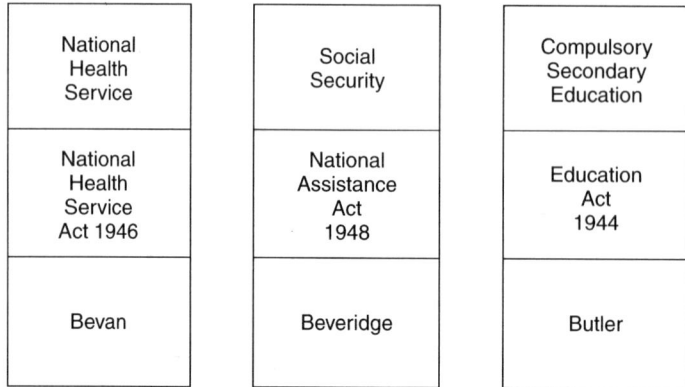

Figure 1.1   The 'Three Pillars' of the welfare state

What is often omitted from such descriptions are the significant role of the Curtis Committee (1946) and the subsequent legislation, the Children Act 1948. Prior to these developments child care was a chaotic mixture of voluntary, charitable and state provision with little or no co-ordination. The Curtis Committee argued that this should be replaced by a unified and comprehensive system of child care. This led to the establishment of a network of local children's officers (the forerunners of today's field social workers) and residential services. The major aim was to give children in care the same level of care and the same opportunities and benefits as children brought up in their families. Although the success of this venture has clearly been very limited, these attempts to take away the stigma of residential care were important in setting the expectations – establishing the ideal to be aimed for. Instead of accepting residential care as inevitably a second rate alternative to family care, this development gave the motivation to strive for as much equality as possible.

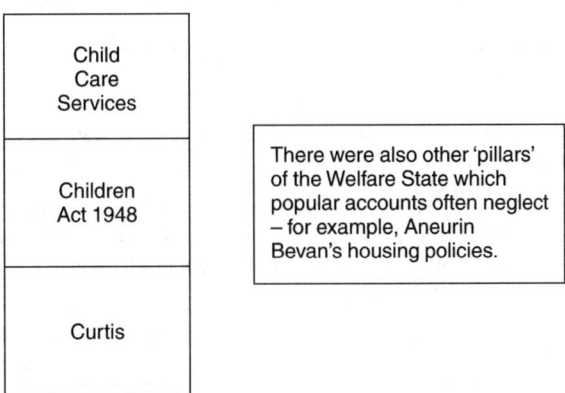

Figure 1.2 The 'fourth pillar' of the welfare state

The Children's Departments established by the Children Act 1948 were specialist agencies which offered services to children and their families. They were to survive only until 1971, when an era of 'genericism' in social work began as a result of the Seebohm Report (1968) in England and Wales and the Kilbrandon Report (1968) in Scotland. As a result of the report of the Seebohm Committee (established by the government of the day to review the provision of social welfare services), 1971 saw the development of Social Services Departments in Wales and England; Social Work Departments had been established in Scotland in 1968. These generic, multipurpose welfare departments incorporated the Children's Departments and produced a situation in which residential child care services became part of a much bigger, more bureaucratic and more hierarchical organisation which offered services to all client groups.

Also a feature of the 1970s was the growth of 'Observation and Assessment' centres. The primary role of these residential units was to provide a period of short-term care during which time a detailed assessment of the child's needs and circumstances would be undertaken in order to establish future plans. For many children this was the entry point to care. Within six to eight weeks it was hoped that residential care staff, together with some input from the field social worker and others (for example, a child psychiatrist), could produce helpful plans for the child concerned. The main options were:

- return to the family home with ongoing support to deal with identified problems and conflicts;
- placement with foster carers;
- transfer to a longer term residential unit (either a 'family group home' – a small-scale residential centre – or a 'CHE' – a community home with education on the premises, a more structured regime); and
- referral to a more specialised resource.

These Observation and Assessment Centres were designed to cater for a wide range of children in need of care, by identifying their problems and needs and thereby formulating the most appropriate form of help for them. This was a reflection of The Children and Young Persons Act 1969 and its philosophy of not segregating young offenders from other youngsters in need of care. The 1969 Act promoted the idea of young offenders as being 'troublesome' because they are 'troubled' – that is, we should see them more as children *with* problems rather than children *as* problems. As a result of this, Observation and Assessment Centres also tended to act as remand centres and provided reports and recommendations for the youth court (or 'juvenile' court as it was then called).

Exercise 1.1

Before continuing to wade through this potted history of child care, take some time out to consider what you have read so far.

1. Do the developments you have read here cast any light on any aspect of your work?
2. Do you feel residential child care is any less stigmatised now than it was in earlier times?
3. Do your views on this matter differ from those of your colleagues?

These are some of the questions which arise. Jot down your views and feelings on 'the story so far' and try to use these, when you get a chance, in discussion with your colleagues.

Residential care proved to be a popular option in the 1970s, as a reliance on fostering tended to decline. However, in the 1980s, the numbers of children in care declined quite significantly and, in particular, the numbers in residential care fell by two thirds (see Figure 1.3). Sir William Utting, in his review of residential child care (1991), explains these falling numbers in the following terms:

> Prevailing values in child care turned firmly in favour of placing children in families and this was also usually perceived as much the cheaper course. The reduction also reflected changes in practice, such as the care order in criminal proceedings falling into disuse. (p. 7)

He also felt that these reductions reflected the success of preventative work geared towards avoiding the need for children to come into care.

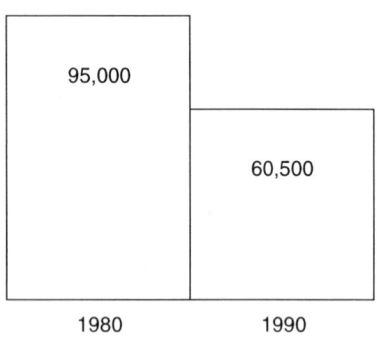

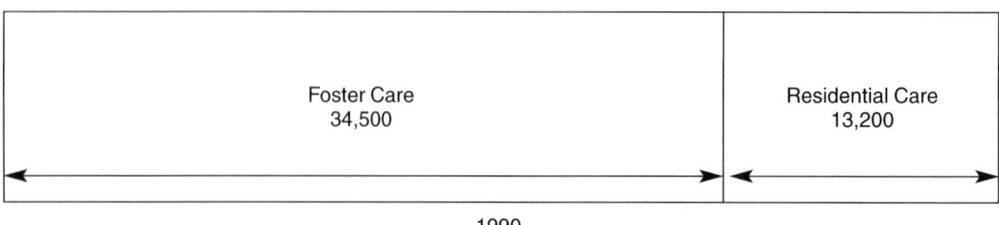

Figure 1.3   Based on figures from Utting (1991)

While this decline in numbers was taking place there were other significant developments happening in child care. Child care law had become a complex muddle of various pieces of legislation and there was considerable concern that the system of child care policy and practice was not providing an adequate service for children in need, particularly in England and Wales. This gave rise to the publication, in 1984, of a report by the House of Commons Social Services Select Committee entitled 'Children in Care' (although more commonly known as 'The Short Report', named after the chair of the committee). This report recommended a major review of child care law and policy in order to find an approach to child care which was less complex, confusing and contradictory.

This was the first step towards what was to become the Children Act 1989 – a major overhaul in England and Wales of child care policy, provision and practice based on clearer and simpler principles. The implementation of this Act (in October, 1991) has had a major impact on child care in general and residential work in particular. It is therefore worth examining the key principles of the Children Act 1989 and their implications for group care with children and young people. However, these issues will not be tackled in any great depth as they are covered by a range of government publications and other texts (see the 'Guide to further learning' section at the end of Chapter 1). But, before looking more closely at the Children Act 1989, we need to consider another major development which occurred in the late 1980s, namely the publication of the Wagner Report: 'Residential Care: A Positive Choice'.

This report was the outcome of an independent review of residential care commissioned by the UK government in December 1985. Its brief was to:

> review the role of residential care and the range of services given in statutory, voluntary and private residential establishments within the personal social services in England and Wales, to consider, having regard to the practical constraints and other relevant developments what changes, if any, are required to enable the residential care sector to respond effectively to changing social needs. (Wagner, 1988, p. 1)

The report recognised the low morale in residential care and the low status ascribed to the work. Indeed, one of the principles of good practice identified in the report is that: 'Residential staff are the major resource and should be valued as such. The importance of their contribution needs to be recognised and enhanced' (p. 114).

In total, the report made 45 recommendations and has been seen as a charter of rights and good practice. The principles and recommendations (pp. 114–19) are worth consulting (see also the 'Guide to further learning' section at the end of the chapter).

The current framework

The Children Act 1989

The current child care framework in England and Wales is based on a number of key principles which are intended as a guide to the development of more helpful and constructive forms of policy and practice. Let us now consider each of the main principles in turn.

1. *Parental responsibility*

Previous legislation was perhaps more concerned with parental rights than responsibilities. The current emphasis, however, is very much on parental responsibility. For social care staff, this means working *with* parents, rather than *instead of* them. Parents do not lose their responsibility, even when their child is subject to a care order and is living away from home.

2. *Public and private law combined*

Under the Children Act 1989, the matters relating to matrimonial and related court proceedings (private law) are dealt with in accordance with the same principles as other matters relating to the protection and welfare of children (public law). There is no longer a distinction between the two.

3. *Paramountcy of the child's welfare*

Basically this means that at all times the welfare of the child (or children) must be the first priority. Other matters, however important, must not be allowed to get in the way of this overriding principle – the welfare of the child first and foremost.

4. *Balance of rights*

This refers to the balance of rights between parents and their children. Families have a right to go about their business without undue interference from social services workers or others. However, children and young people also have a right to protection and adequate care. We therefore have to tread a fine line between the two sets of rights.

5. *Only positive intervention*

Following on from principle No. 4 is a duty to ensure, as far as possible, that any steps taken by social services, particularly in relation to court orders and compulsory care, are to be of positive benefit to the child. This places a much heavier burden on social services staff to justify why court action is felt to be necessary.

6. *Partnership*

This echoes principle No. 1 and the need to share parental responsibility with natural parents rather than take over such responsibilities. This means working closely together to draw up plans and to put them into effect. Partnership will be a major theme of Chapter 3, and will also feature significantly in Chapter 5.

7. *Statutory versus voluntary involvement*

Social services have a duty to support families, where necessary, by providing a range of services (for example, day care). This is a preventative role (to prevent family breakdown and/or harm to children) and is carried out on a voluntary basis. However, it is recognised that there is also a remedial role – that is, to remedy a harmful situation for a child. Such situations should be dealt with on a voluntary basis but, if necessary, this should become 'statutory' – that is, by recourse to the law and a possible court order.

8. *Equality of opportunity*

The Act requires social services and others to take greater account of equality issues in relation to race and culture, language, gender, sexual orientation and disability. These issues will be addressed more specifically later in this chapter and will also underpin the book as a whole.

9. *Delay is harmful*

As we shall see in Chapter 3, planning is a key element of child care. Delay in the decision-making processes can therefore prove to be very harmful in the long run as well as causing additional distress in the short term. This principle is particularly applicable to court proceedings, where delay has been a major problem in the past.

10. *Significant harm*

Where children are felt to be experiencing significant harm, or where there is a likelihood of such harm taking place, steps must be taken to remedy this situation. This will be discussed in more detail in Chapter 5.

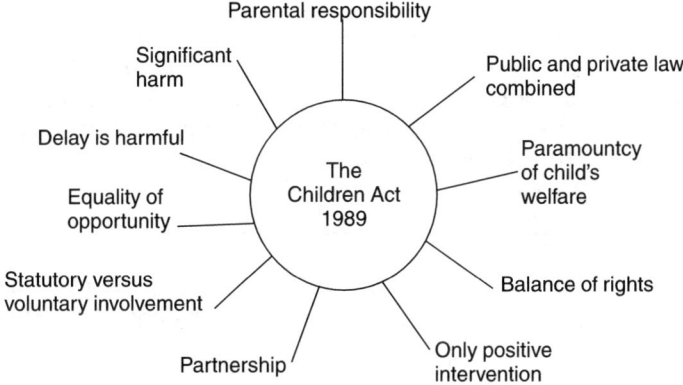

Figure 1.4   The principles underpinning the Children Act 1989

There are, of course, many other themes and principles which can be found to apply in the Act, but these are some of the main features which help us to understand the philosophy which acts as the basis of this major piece of legislation. They give us the basis for understanding the 'spirit of the Act'.

The Care Standards Act 2000

This act is a key part of policy and practice in residential care. It lays down the criteria that children's homes must meet in order to satisfy the requirements of registration. It sets down the broad terms governing the registration and inspection of residential provision for children and young people. The policies and procedures of your employing organization are likely to be strongly influenced by this piece of legislation. And, when the inspectors come to visit, a major part of their role will be to ensure that the requirements of this Act are being met.

The Human Rights Act 1998

This Act, implemented in October 2000, made the European Convention on Human Rights (ECHR) a part of UK law. This means that people who believe that their human rights are being infringed can now, in most cases, seek justice in the UK's domestic courts without having to go to the expense and trouble of taking their case to the European Court of Human Rights in Strasbourg.

In principle, this Act has a number of implications for group care staff. For example, under the ECHR, there is a right to 'security of the person'. This therefore has implications in terms of the use of physical restraint (see Chapter 7). It is important, in order to comply with this law, that any such restraint is i) necessary and ii) proportionate (that is, not excessive in the circumstances).

Having sketched out some of the major elements in the history of residential child care and having now outlined some of the major principles of the current framework, it will shortly be time to move on and consider the value base of our work. But, before doing this, there is a further exercise for you to do to consolidate your understanding of how the law applies to your work.

Exercise 1.2

Look again at the ten principles of the Children Act 1989 outlined above (and depicted in Figure 1.4). Then try and relate each of these to an aspect of your work. Can you think of any ways in which you can see links between elements of your day-to-day work and the ten principles? Use a separate sheet of paper to give brief details. Don't worry if you can't complete all ten (some principles are easier to apply than others) but do come back to the exercise later. It would also be useful for you to compare notes with colleagues.

If you are interested in finding out more about the legal and policy context of your work, you can make use of the 'Guide to further learning' section at the end of this chapter.

The value base

Good child care practice requires a commitment to certain values, such as the importance of giving children a fair and reasonable chance to make something of their lives in society; a general humanitarian value of caring and compassion; the recognition of a child's right to be protected from harm, and so on. It is important that we should be aware of these basic values and avoid the temptation of cynically dismissing them or minimising their importance. It is often from these values that we get our motivation and a clearer vision of our aims and objectives.

In addition to these more general values, however, there is the specific issue of equality of opportunity and, flowing from this, a host of issues relating to the development of anti-discriminatory practice. These are difficult issues in two senses. On the one hand, they are difficult due to their complexity and subtle intricacies. On the other hand, they are difficult because they are contentious and can often challenge our own beliefs and values, our assumptions, and indeed the very basis of our view of the world. This being the case, it is therefore very important that we clarify the key elements of anti-discriminatory practice and explain why good practice must be based on such principles of equality. We begin by examining the concept of 'social structure'.

Social divisions and social structure

Individuals and groups interact and inter-relate in society in a wide variety of ways. But this variety does not occur at random or in a totally unpredictable way; there are constants which are detectable. It is in this sense that society is said to be 'structured'. This structure is best understood in terms of 'social divisions' – the significant ways in which society is divided up according to social categories. There are very many such social divisions, but the main ones tend to be seen as: class, race, gender, age and disability, although language, culture, religion and sexual identity are increasingly receiving attention.

But these divisions turn out to be very significant in terms of opportunities afforded to members of each of the groupings. Indeed, inequality and relative disadvantage are central features of the social structure and the social divisions that go to make it up. For example, disabled people are often excluded from participating in mainstream social activities because of inadequate access facilities or other social barriers. As a result of this, disabled people have a decidedly unequal relationship with their able-bodied counterparts. Such inequality is often reinforced by prejudice and discrimination, and can therefore be seen as a very negative, destructive and oppressive force in society – one we would not wish to be party to or condone. The prejudice and discrimination associated with class have long been recognised in social work and social care. The impact of poverty, poor housing and so on, on people's lives has received a great deal of coverage and attention. However, it is only relatively recently that other forms of discrimination have established themselves on the agenda.

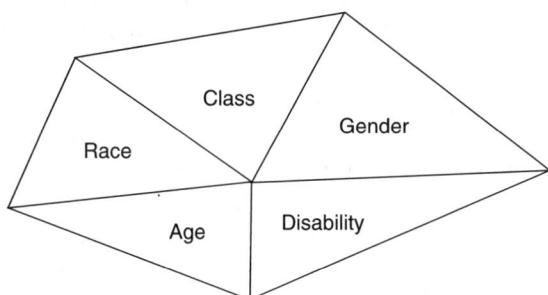

Figure 1.5 Major social divisions

Issues of race and gender made a major impact first, as racism and sexism became recognised as significant problems. More recently, age and disability have featured more prominently and the terms 'ageism' and 'disablism' have been coined to describe the discrimination and oppression associated with these two social divisions. Ageism is usually used to refer to the problems experienced by older people as a result of negative attitudes towards old age. However, we should note that the same concept can be seen to apply to children – for example, in the way that they can be abused, have their rights denied or be treated as the 'possessions' of their parents.

Another point to note in relation to these social divisions is that they are not mutually exclusive. That is, it is often the case that people are subjected to more than one form of discrimination at the same time – a case of 'multiple oppressions'. For example, a black woman is likely to experience racism as well as sexism. Such forms of discrimination are not distinct entities, unrelated to one another. Rather, they are best seen as 'dimensions of experience' (Thompson, 2003a).

The fact that we have an unequal social structure which stacks the odds against certain groups of people in society has major implications for social work and social care in general and child care in particular. It is the recognition of many of these implications which has contributed to the development of anti-discriminatory practice – that is, forms of practice which actively seek to challenge and undermine discrimination and oppression. Let us now look at the basics of what this entails.

Anti-discriminatory practice

One of the principles of anti-discriminatory practice is that discrimination is not simply a personal or individual matter, but actually reflects the way society is structured (the social divisions referred to above). For example, sexism and racism are not just matters of personal prejudice – they are reflections of how society is organised.

The main implication of this is that we cannot simply say 'I am not racist' or 'I am not sexist', as if it were purely a matter of personal attitudes. If we take this approach we are ignoring two key issues:

> 1. Racism and sexism can be 'institutional'. That is, they are built into the way an organisation or service operates. For example, black children are over-represented in compulsory care but black people are under-represented in supportive services. We can therefore detect that there is something inherently discriminatory about the policies or services rather than simply the actions of a bigoted minority.

> 2. Because discrimination is a social and institutional matter as well as a personal one, its influence can be subtle and pervasive and thereby affect our actions without our realising it. For example, the language we use can unwittingly reinforce racist or sexist stereotypes (using 'girl' to refer to an adult woman or 'black' as a negative term – 'It was a black day' and so on – see Thompson, 2003b).

Another way of putting this is to say: 'If you're not part of the solution, you must be part of the problem' (Thompson, 2001). That is, as we live in the context of a racist and sexist society, then our actions will either challenge and undermine these forms of discrimination, or reinforce and condone them by allowing them to go unchecked. This is why we talk of *anti*-racism and *anti*-sexism rather than *non*-racism and *non*-sexism; there is no middle ground, no neutral territory. As women are oppressed by sexism and black people by racism, we can respond in one of two ways. We can play our part in tackling such discrimination and oppression, or we can turn our back on it and allow it to continue. Another analogy we could use is that we must swim against the tide of discrimination. If we do not swim against it, we will be carried along with it. This is what we mean by saying that good practice must be *anti*-discriminatory practice. Working in an anti-discriminatory way is therefore not an 'optional extra'. It is a fundamental and essential aspect of good child care practice.

The examples we have concentrated on here have been those of racism and sexism and these are indeed major issues. However, we should also bear in mind that anti-discriminatory practice applies to all forms of discrimination, including age, disability, sexual orientation and so on. Furthermore, we should bear in mind that children and young people in group care are often subject to discrimination *because* they are in group care.

Exercise 1.3

Anti-discriminatory practice is based on a number of key concepts, some of which are listed below. The aim of this exercise is to give you the opportunity to make sure you understand these terms and are able to begin to relate them to your work. Your task is to write down a short definition of each of the concepts on a separate piece of paper. Use a dictionary if you want to, but beware the temptation to simply copy out the dictionary definition. It is important that you write down *your* definition – that is, one that makes sense to you.

1 Prejudice
2 Discrimination
3 Stereotype
4 Equality of opportunity
5 Racism
6 Sexism
7 Diversity

Having clarified why anti-discriminatory practice is so important in social work and social care in general, there are two main tasks that remain for us to tackle:

1. How do these issues apply to child care work in particular?
2. What practical steps can we take to ensure that we undertake our work in an anti-discriminatory way?

However, before we do tackle them, I want to make some brief comments about a new approach to discrimination issues which is steadily becoming very well established, namely the diversity approach.

Diversity

Literally, diversity means 'variety'. However, the term is increasingly being used to refer to an approach to discrimination issues which emphasises the value of diversity – that is, an approach which recognises that it is a good thing that we are not all the same, that we have variety of culture, background, perspective and so on, all of which enriches us. The diversity approach is based on the idea that, instead of people feeling frightened of the unknown and having a tendency to discriminate against people who are perceived to be different from ourselves, we should work towards being much more positive about the advantages and benefits that come from having a diverse society.

When people talk about the need to 'value diversity', what they are referring to is the recognition that people's differences should be looked upon positively wherever possible and should not be the basis of unfair discrimination. When working with children and young people in group care, we should therefore be careful not to fall into the trap of seeing differences as problems. It is important that we remain open-minded about people as part of a process of valuing diversity.

Discrimination and child care

The effects of discrimination on children and young people can be of extreme proportions, producing children who are very unhappy and distressed and who may manifest this in their behaviour or their attitudes towards others. Perhaps one of the most significant aspects of this is the child or young person's attitude towards him- or herself. This is what is known as the 'self-image', the psychological picture we have of ourselves. A negative self-image leads to a lack of confidence and low self-esteem and this, in turn, can lead to fewer opportunities in life. Thus, the psychological impact of discrimination (for example, through racial violence) can make worse the social disadvantages (for example, poorer career prospects due to institutional racism within the employment system). These issues of self-esteem and identity will be considered in more detail in Chapter 2.

As children grow up they are given 'messages' from the people around them about what is normal, how to behave, what their roles are and so on. By looking at the social context in which children grow up we can see how the structure of society (the social divisions) gives different 'messages' to children according to where they are located in society – their gender, racial or ethnic background and so on. For example, boys are taught to be tough and to keep their feelings to themselves, while girls are expected to be gentle and caring. These restrictive expectations can be very oppressive for children and can cause problems in terms of boys not feeling able to grieve at a time of loss or girls not feeling able to speak out when they are unhappy about something.

This latter point is particularly relevant to sexual abuse, for example. There are a number of gender issues which apply here:

- the vast majority of perpetrators are male;
- the vast majority of victims are female;
- feminists have rightly argued that popular conceptions of sexuality portray women and girls as if their main role is to satisfy men's needs; and
- victims of sexual abuse often feel unable to speak out against the perpetrators, who are in a position of power over them.

These points will be raised again in Chapter 5 when the topic of child abuse is discussed, and guidelines for further study of these issues are given in the 'Guide to further learning' section at the end of that chapter.

These are just some of the many aspects of discrimination that can be seen to apply to child care. Very many more examples could have been given but the aim is not to give you a thorough grounding in these issues. Instead, the aim is a broader one – to help to sensitise you to these matters, so that you can 'take them on board' and weave them into your practice with children and young people. In other words, it is not just the 'knowledge base' that you need.

What is most important is the commitment to developing anti-discriminatory practice by changing our own attitudes, values and behaviour. With this commitment comes motivation to develop the necessary knowledge base. But, without this commitment, the knowledge base is useless. As Figure 1.6 shows, anti-discriminatory practice requires us to develop on three fronts: knowledge, skills and values.

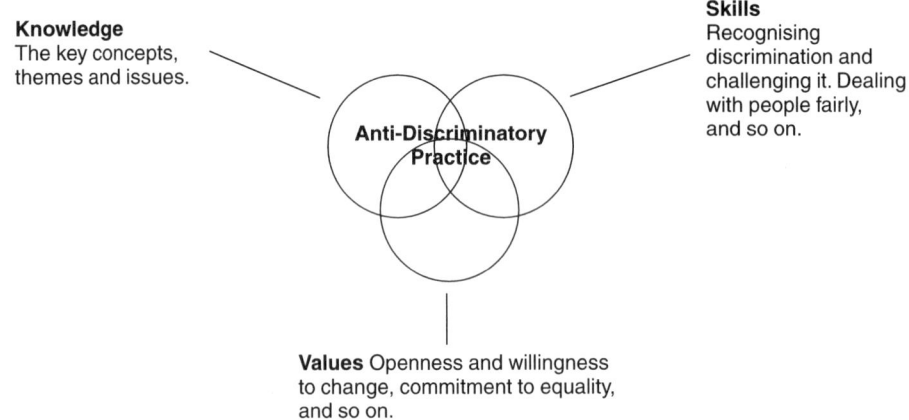

Figure 1.6   The Knowledge Skills Values framework

Guidelines for action

What we need to do now is strike a balance. At the one extreme, I could provide pages and pages of detailed practice guidance for developing anti-discriminatory practice in child care. Realistically, though, we do not have the space to do this. And, besides, there is considerable value in trying to work some of these things out for yourself (together with your colleagues). On the other hand, I could leave you to work it all out for yourself; I could leave you to draw your own links between the issues raised and your day-to-day work with children and young people. However, this would not be very fair or helpful either. Consequently, the balance we are striving for is this: some broad principles and guidelines will be provided, but you will need to go through the process of relating these to your own work and building up for yourself (with the aid of colleagues and further training, of course) your own approach to anti-discriminatory practice. What follows, then, are some basic principles to help you to challenge inequality and disadvantage by working within an anti-discriminatory framework:

1. *Beware of stereotypical assumptions*

Stereotypes are dangerous and misleading. You should be wary of making assumptions about black children, children from a different religious background or who speak a different language and so on. Also, you need to make sure you are not reinforcing stereotypical gender roles when you are dealing with children, colleagues, parents and so on.

2. *Don't exclude fathers*

Traditional wisdom sees bringing up children as primarily a mother's role. We need to be careful to ensure that we do not reinforce the sexism in this by focusing our attentions on the mother's role and thus marginalising or excluding the father, stepfather or cohabitee.

3. *Develop self-awareness*

Are there any elements of prejudice or discrimination in our own thoughts, feelings and values? What steps do we need to take to overcome this? Who do we trust enough to help us achieve this? These are all important questions we need to address if our commitment to equality and fairness is to be more than an empty gesture.

4. *Avoid discriminatory language*

The prevalence and potency of discrimination are reflected in the language we use. We need to become sensitive to our use of language and avoid words or phrases which reinforce sexism, racism, and so on. For example, words like 'chairman' have the effect of excluding and marginalising women. They reinforce the notion that 'It's a man's world'. (Please note, however, that the relationship between discrimination and language is a complex one. Beware of oversimplified approaches that simply involve a list of 'taboo' words that should not be used – see Thompson, 2003b.)

5. *Challenge discrimination*

It is not enough to tackle discrimination within our own language, thought and behaviour. We also need to ensure that we do not allow discrimination to go unchecked on the part of others or within policies and organisational routines. Anti-discrimination is not served by turning our backs on instances of discrimination.

6. *Encourage a positive identity*

Children and young people should be encouraged to feel proud of their identity in terms of their race and culture, gender, class, religion and so on. Children and young people will often be found to have internalised the notion that different equals inferior. Steps can, and should, be taken to encourage a positive identity free of any feelings of inferiority.

7. *Be wary of humour*

A good sense of humour is, of course, an important ingredient in successful child care. However, we need to be aware that it is also an important and effective vehicle for discrimination. Humour is often discriminatory (for example, sexist jokes or jokes about Irishmen) and can be very cruel. This type of humour needs to be discouraged but without other harmless forms of humour being discouraged.

8. *Remember that children are people first*

It is often forgotten that children have human rights and should not be treated as the 'possessions' of their parents. The Children Act 1989 has gone some way towards dispelling this notion. Many of the problems experienced by children in care would not have occurred (for example, 'pindown', an unacceptable means of controlling or disciplining children – see Levy and Kahan, 1991) if this principle had been to the fore. This principle also applies to children with disabilities – they are children first and disabled second.

9. *Avoid isolation*

Developing anti-discriminatory practice is not just a task for you personally. It is something which all care staff and all social welfare organisations are going to have to strive for, especially in view of the requirements of the Children Act 1989. Anti-discriminatory practice is complex, difficult and demanding. You therefore need to make sure you are supported and accompanied in your attempts to achieve your aims.

10. *Work towards empowerment*

Empowerment is a concept which is central to anti-discriminatory practice. It involves helping people gain power and control over their own lives. Children can be helped to overcome some of the disadvantages imposed on them by the social structure and the inequality, disadvantage and discrimination inherent in it, as indeed can parents and staff. Discrimination 'disempowers' people. A key part of our task, therefore, is to seek to redress the balance.

These are some of the fundamental building blocks of anti-discriminatory practice. The task that faces you now is a crucial one – to start the process of relating the theory you have read about here to the reality of your own practice. (Remember the Kolb 'learning cycle' you were introduced to earlier.) Exercise 1.4 is intended to help you with this process, but the exercise will not be enough on its own – you will need to keep coming back to these issues. They will feature at various stages in the other parts of the book and this will, I hope, help you to integrate anti-discriminatory practice into your work.

Exercise 1.4

Consider each of the ten principles outlined above and try to relate them, one by one, to work situations. Try to think of concrete examples of how each principle can be applied to your work. Once again this shouldn't be an isolated activity. Jot down your ideas first but then you could compare notes with your colleagues and take the opportunity of learning from each other.

Conclusion

It is increasingly being recognised that group care with children and young people is both a very demanding undertaking and a very important one. Understanding the historical context and the value base can help to ensure that it is done effectively and from an informed basis. The historical context is particularly important in terms of how it has helped to shape the current legislative framework of the Children Act 1989.

The value base is also of major significance for, as we have seen, good practice must be anti-discriminatory practice. However, there is a danger here that progress on these matters may be blocked. The obstacle I have in mind is the tendency amongst some people to deny or minimise the significance of discrimination and disadvantage: 'It isn't a problem around here'. Webb and Tossell (1991) make a similar point in relation to racism in particular:

> Racism is an immensely complex subject and one which perhaps, more than any other is likely to evoke strong feelings whenever it is raised. People may feel strongly because they have experienced and continue to experience the effects of racism in their everyday lives, or they may feel angry simply because of the social injustice of racism. Some individuals may feel threatened and act defensively whenever the matter is mentioned for fear of their own actions being criticised or condemned. Yet others will remain confused and uncertain about an issue they feel to be inflated in importance since it has barely touched their lives. (p. 64)

It is the people who feel that the importance of racism as an issue has been inflated who are in danger of failing to grasp just how oppressive issues like racism and sexism can be for those who fall victim to them.

In relation to racism, this danger applies most of all in those areas where numbers of black people are relatively low. The comment frequently made is that 'We don't have many black people in our area'. Unfortunately, this view misses a number of points:

- the numbers of black people living locally are often underestimated;
- this approach has the underlying message 'our services are for white people only'. If black people were to need services, staff would be unprepared;
- issues of race and culture, as emphasised in the Children Act 1989, apply to many other ethnic groups who encounter discrimination – Jewish people, travellers, Irish people in the UK and so on. Even when dealing with white children, awareness of racism has a significant part to play in terms of challenging racist attitudes and behaviours on their part.

(For a discussion of how some efforts to promote equality have been misguided and sometimes even counterproductive, see Thompson, 2003a, Chapter 5.)

The important point to remember, of course, is: 'if you're not part of the solution, you must be part of the problem'. It is understandable that anxieties about dealing with contentious matters such as racism and sexism could lead us down the path of avoiding the subject whenever possible. But, however understandable this avoidance may be, it is something we cannot afford. The price for those concerned, not least the children and young people we work with, is far too high.

Having now discussed and explored the context and value base of group care, it is time to move on and consider the other important aspects of your work. We begin by examining children's and young people's needs and trying to identify what can be done to meet these needs as far as possible.

Guide to further learning

1. *The historical context*

Adams, R. (1996) *The Personal Social Services*, London, Longman.
Kahan, B. (1994) *Growing Up in Groups*, London, HMSO – now the Stationery Office.

2. *Current issues*

Burton, J. (1993) *The Handbook of Residential Care*, London, Routledge.
Crimmens, D. and Pitts, J. (eds) (2000) *Positive Residential Practice: Learning the Lessons of the 1990s*, Lyme Regis, Russell House Publishing.
Cullen, D. and Lane, M. (2003) *Child Care Law: A Summary of the Law in England and Wales*, 4th edn, London, BAAF.
Evans, D. and Kearney, J. (1996) *Working in Social Care: A Systemic Approach*, Aldershot, Arena.
Foley, P., Roche, J. and Tucker, S. (eds) (2001) *Children in Society: Contemporary Theory, Policy and Practice*, Basingstoke, Palgrave Macmillan.
Watson, J. and Woolf, M. (2003) *Human Rights Act Toolkit*, London, Legal Action Group.
White, R., Carr, P. and Lowe, N. (1990) *A Guide to the Children Act 1989*, London, Butterworth.

3. *Social divisions and social structure*

Abercrombie, N. and Warde, A. with Deem, R., Penna, S., Soothill, K., Urry, J., Sayer, A. and Walby, S. (2000) *Contemporary British Society*, 3rd edn, Oxford, Polity.
Bates, I. and Riseborough, G. (1993) *Youth and Inequality*, Buckingham, Open University Press.
Giddens, A. (2001) Sociology, 4th edn, Cambridge, Polity.

4. *Anti-discriminatory practice*

General texts
Braye, S. and Preston-Shoot, M. (1995) *Empowering Practice in Social Care*, Buckingham, Open University Press.
Dalrymple, J. and Burke, B. (1995) *Anti-Oppressive Practice, Social Care and the Law*, Buckingham, Open University Press.
Thompson, N. (2001) *Anti-Discriminatory Practice*, 3rd edn, Basingstoke, Palgrave Macmillan.
Thompson, N. (2002) *People Skills*, 2nd edn, Basingstoke, Palgrave Macmillan. Chapters 9 and 17.
Thompson, N. (2003) *Promoting Equality: Challenging Discrimination and Oppression*, 2nd edn, Basingstoke, Palgrave Macmillan.

Anti-racism
Ahmad, B. (1990) *Black Perspectives in Social Work*, Birmingham, Venture Press.
CD Project Steering Group (eds) (1991) *Setting the Context for Change*, London, CCETSW.
Dwivedi, K.N. (ed.) (2002) *Meeting the Needs of Ethnic Minority Children: A Handbook for Professionals*, 2nd edn, London, Jessica Kingsley.
Robinson, L. (1995) *Psychology for Social Workers*, London, Routledge.

Anti-sexism

Elliot, F.R. (1996) *Gender, Family and Society*, London, Macmillan – now Palgrave Macmillan.

Grimwood, C. and Popplestone, R. (1993) *Women, Management and Care*, London, Macmillan – now Palgrave Macmillan.

Gruber, C. and Stepanov, H. (eds) (2002) *Gender in Social Work: Promoting Equality*, Lyme Regis, Russell House Publishing.

Langan, M. and Day, L (eds) (1992) *Women, Oppression and Social Work: Issues in Anti-Discriminatory Practice*, London, Routledge.

Thompson, N. (1995) 'Men and Anti-Sexism,' *British Journal of Social Work*, 25(4).

Anti-disablism

Campbell, J. and Oliver, M. (1996) *Disability Politics: Understanding Our Past, Changing Our Future*, London, Routledge.

Morris, J. (1991) *Pride Against Prejudice*, London, Women's Press.

Oliver, M. and Sapey, B. (1999) *Social Work with Disabled People*, 2nd edn, Basingstoke, Palgrave Macmillan.

Oliver, M. (1990) *The Politics of Disablement*, Basingstoke, Palgrave Macmillan.

Oliver, M. (1996) *Understanding Disability: From Theory to Practice*, Basingstoke, Palgrave Macmillan.

Chapter 2

Understanding Children's Needs

Introduction

We all have basic needs for survival such as food, water and shelter. There can be little dispute about this, but there are two areas in relation to human needs which are subject to considerable debate and disagreement. These are:

1. Apart from the basic survival needs, are there other human needs which are common to us all? If so, what are they?
2. What specific needs do children have, as distinct from adults?

My aim is not to give definitive answers to these questions, but it is to be hoped that this chapter will give us a clearer picture of children's (and young people's) needs and their crucial relevance to good practice in group care.

The chapter is divided into four main sections. The first looks at different theories of needs. Various approaches to this topic have been developed over the years and each of them casts at least some light on the question of children's needs. The second section considers child development. The various dimensions or 'strands' of child development are charted and the implications of these for our work with children and young people are outlined. The third section focuses on one particular aspect of child development, namely identity formation. The concept of identity is a unifying theme which helps us make sense of some of the complexities of child development and children's needs. The fourth section addresses the issues associated with how children cope with stress, change, rejection and loss, and how you and other child care workers can help them in this process.

As with each of the eight chapters, we end with a 'Guide to further learning'. Here you will find a range of possible sources for you to draw on to help you get the most out of your learning.

Theories of need

There have been a number of influential texts on the subject of human needs, including some which focus particularly on the needs of children, for example Kellmer Pringle (1986) and Berry (1972).

Berry (1972) divides needs into three main categories and these are:

1. Physical: food, clothes, shelter and so on;
2. Emotional and social: love, consistency, firmness, a sense of security and continuity;
3. Intellectual: environmental stimulation, opportunities for play, achievement and discovery of oneself in relation to the world.

She also points out that these needs, and their satisfaction, often tend to overlap. For example, giving food is also usually about giving love, and so physical need is met at the same time as an emotional and social need.

A common criticism of this type of approach is that it is too generalised. The concepts are so broad and vague as to have little direct applicability to guiding our day-to-day practice with children. For example, are child care workers expected to 'love' the children they work with? What does love mean in this context?

Consider also the need for consistency. What does this amount to? How does it differ from a stifling uniformity or a misleading impression that adult caregivers will respond according to a set pattern, regardless of differing circumstances? (see Thompson, 2002b, for a discussion of some of these issues). These broad conceptions of need may well be a good starting point, but we need to recognise their limitations. They will take us only so far in our understanding of children and their needs.

One of the main problems with these 'standardised' approaches to the notion of need is that they fail to take sufficient account of differences between children – for example, in terms of race, culture and gender. For example, all children need food but what is seen as acceptable food depends on a range of racial, ethnic or religious factors. (This is an example of the significance of diversity, a point to which we shall return below.)

This also applies to emotional and social needs. For example, girls subjected to the oppressions of sexism and black children of both genders, similarly affected by racism, are likely to have different emotional and social experiences from white boys and therefore different needs – for example, the need to be supported through experiences of harassment. In considering children's needs we therefore have to take account not only of what they have in common with other children, but also of what is specific to their social grouping and, indeed, what is unique to them as individuals.

In addition, it is important to remember that needs are linked to purposes and intentions. The key phrase is 'in order to …' – for example, we need food in order to feel secure and valued. These purposes or intentions can then be seen to be inter-related or embedded in layers. This is illustrated in Figure 2.1.

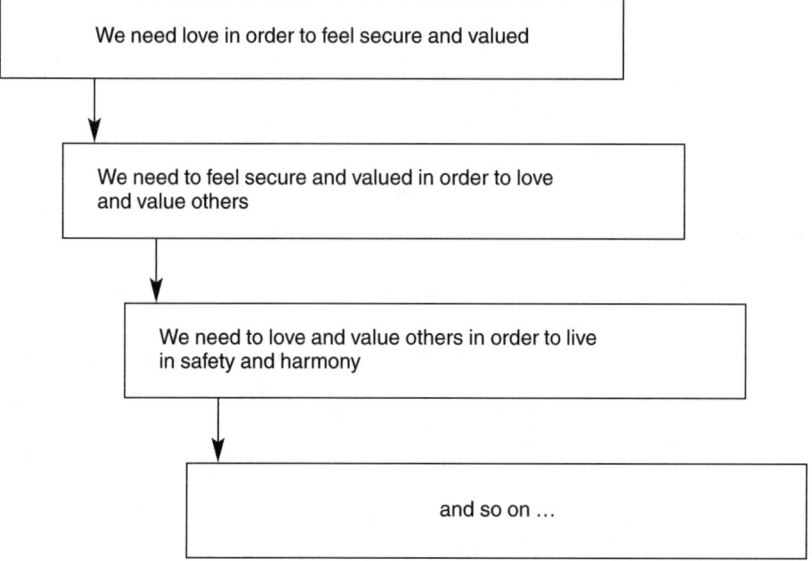

Figure 2.1   'Layers' of need

In looking at the needs of the children we work with, it is therefore essential to bear in mind the following factors:

- need is not absolute and is related to factors such as class, race and gender;
- need is related to purpose or intention. The key phrase is 'in order to …';
- needs tend to be inter-related and 'layered'. They therefore have to be seen as part of a pattern, rather than in isolation.

These factors are important aspects of assessment, and so I shall return to them in Chapter 3. The notion of 'layering' is also an important part of another influential theory of human needs, that of Abraham Maslow. Maslow (1973) argued that there is a 'hierarchy' of needs involving five levels, from the most basic needs for survival to the highest of 'self-actualisation'. These are shown in Figure 2.2

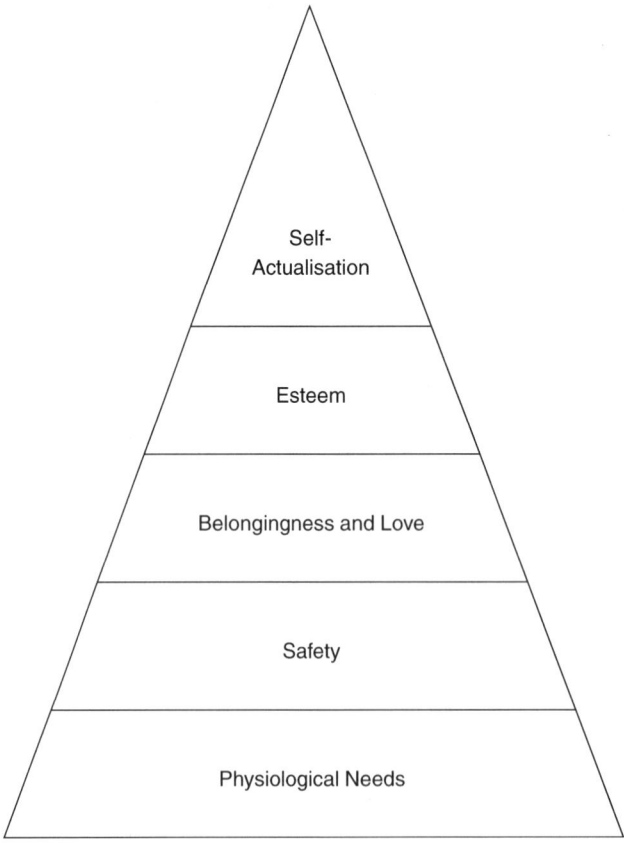

Figure 2.2   Maslow's 'hierarchy of needs'

The basic principle underlying Maslow's theory is that we cannot progress from one level to another without our needs first being met at the lower level. That is, we cannot be safe unless our physiological needs (air, food, water and so on) are satisfied; we cannot experience love and belongingness unless we feel safe. The ultimate 'pinnacle' of this hierarchy is 'self-actualisation', the realisation of our full potential through finding or constructing a coherent framework of meaning and value which allows us to achieve a sense of personal fulfilment. As with other frameworks of human need, Maslow's hierarchy gives us a useful starting point for making sense of children's needs, but is far from adequate or complete in its own right. It leaves very many questions unanswered.

Maslow's hierarchy of needs model is not geared specifically towards children but none the less offers a useful framework for understanding, to a certain extent at least, the needs of a particular child or children. The fourth level of need, that of esteem, is one to which we shall return below.

One further aspect of children's needs which merits our attention is the need for protection, specifically protection from abuse. This is a need which is fully recognised in law and government guidance and forms a significant element in the foundations of the Children Act 1989. Child protection is indeed an issue of major importance both for child care professionals in general and for group child care workers in particular. Consequently, child protection forms the basis of a whole chapter. Chapter 5 is therefore devoted specifically to issues of 'Dealing with Abuse'.

We shall shortly be moving on to broaden our understanding of children's needs by examining the basics of child development. However, before we do so, it is important to try to relate theory to practice. Exercise 2.1 has been designed to help you begin to do this. You are therefore advised to spend some time tackling the exercise before beginning your study of the next section.

Exercise 2.1

This is a case study exercise. It involves choosing a particular child that you work with and considering what his or her needs are and, if these needs are not being met, what has to happen to solve this situation. Use a separate sheet of paper, divide it into two columns and use the following two headings:

Identified Need   *How are these needs met? or What has to change to ensure that they are met?*

Note: This can be a very simple and effortless exercise if you tackle it in a very broad and general level – but then you won't get much benefit from doing the exercise. It is better to base your answers on the concepts and framework you have studied in this section (for example, by considering factors of class, race and gender). In this way you will both develop your practice and consolidate your learning.

Child development

Rutter (1975) argues that:

> children are developing organisms so that assessment needs to be made in the context of a developmental framework. This means that clinicians must have a good knowledge and understanding of child development, both normal and abnormal. Children behave differently at different ages and it is necessary to know what behaviour should be expected at each age (p. 16)

This, of course, has major implications for how we deal with children, how we treat them in relation to the perceived level of development which they are presumed to have reached. Failing to gauge this level appropriately can mean that our attempts to work with a particular child or children are doomed to failure. For example, we may expect too much of a child and thereby set him or her up to fail or, conversely, we could set our expectations too low and thereby produce boredom and a lack of motivation. Child development is a complex and detailed subject matter and so we have no hope of covering it here in anything approaching a comprehensive way. I shall none the less be able to cover the basics and give you the opportunity to begin to develop your own knowledge and views of how children develop and the patterns they tend to follow.

I shall begin by looking at some of the traditional 'stage' models of development and consider their weakness of relying on largely biological explanations. From this we shall move on to examine other strands of development, particularly the psychological and the social.

Stage models of development

There are a number of theorists who have developed 'stage' models – that is, theoretical explanations of development as a progression through a number of stages or phases. Perhaps the most well-known of these is that of Erikson (1977), who wrote of the 'Eight Ages of Man'. He saw each of us as passing through eight key stages throughout the human lifespan. At each of these stages we have the task of integrating the demands of the new stage into our experience gained during the previous stages. That is, the task is to adjust to the new stage. Figure 2.3 outlines these eight stages.

1.	**Basic Trust** vs. **Basic Mistrust**	The young baby needs to learn to trust first parents and then others.
2.	**Autonomy** vs. **Shame and Doubt**	The young child needs to learn to think and act for him/herself, to develop self-control.
3.	**Initiative** vs. **Guilt**	The growing child needs to begin to move towards independence and use initiative, albeit in a limited way.
4.	**Industry** vs. **Inferiority**	The young school child needs to learn the value and pleasure of achieving tasks.
5.	**Identity** vs. **Role Confusion**	In the early stages of adolescence, a coherent sense of identity needs to be formed in preparation for adulthood.
6.	**Intimacy** vs. **Isolation**	The young adult needs to establish adult relationships and form a new generation of family life.
7.	**Generativity** vs. **Stagnation**	Maturity needs to be characterised by a sense of achievement, productivity and fulfilment.
8.	**Ego Integrity** vs. **Despair**	In the latter stages of life, we need to face up to the reality of death with dignity.

Figure 2.3   Erikson's *Eight Ages of Man*

Erikson's framework is not presented as an ideal model. It is far from ideal, for example in how it neglects significant issues such as race and gender – the fact that he uses the term 'Eight Ages of *Man*' gives us some clue about this!

The model is presented not as ideal but as typical of the many stage models of child development. They all give a framework of broad, general stages through which children are said to pass. Details of books which describe other such stage models can be found in the

'Guide to further learning' section for those who wish to pursue this further. The main point to note, however, is that there is no definitive model of child development which gives us 'all the answers'. There are various approaches and each of them, like Erikson's, offers a mixture of helpful insights, limitations and pitfalls. In learning about child development, there can be no substitute for reading widely on the subject and making a determined effort to relate the theories and frameworks to our own careful observation and knowledge of children as they grow and develop.

Strands of development

One aspect of the subject which can help us in our learning is the way in which development can be subdivided into different dimensions or 'strands'. As mentioned above, one significant weakness of stage approaches is that they tend to overemphasise the biological dimension of the life cycle at the expense of other key aspects, such as the cognitive, emotional, social or political. The intention in this section, therefore, is to rectify the balance to a certain extent by focusing on each of these additional dimensions in turn.

1. *The cognitive strand*

'Cognitive' is a term used to refer to thinking and thought processes. It relates to memory and the ability to reason or think in abstract terms. Piaget is probably the most well-known theorist in this area of child development. Piaget was also a stage theorist, although his stages related specifically to cognitive development. The main elements of his model are outlined in Figure 2.4.

Stage 1: Sensory motor

| Birth to 2 years |

The young baby begins life with basic sensory reflexes and these are gradually adapted as the child learns to relate sensory experience to the outside world.

Stage 2: The Pre-operational

| 2 to 7 years |

The young child learns many new things but these often remain unconnected, and not part of a wider whole. Language development is also a feature of this stage.

Stage 3: Concrete Operational

| 7 to 12 years |

The child's learning continues but is restricted to the here and now and is concerned with concrete experience.

Stage 4: Formal Operational

| 12 years onwards |

The child develops the capacity for abstract thought and is able to think in a systematic and planned manner.

Figure 2.4   Piaget's stages of development

However, it would be a mistake to see Piaget's theory as just a stage theory. He also introduces a number of concepts which have been extremely influential in education and child care. We do not have space to go into detail about these and so we shall look briefly at only two. (If you want to further your understanding of Piaget's work, there is, of course, guidance about this in the 'Guide to further learning' section.)

i. Assimilation and accommodation

As part of their learning, children develop 'schemas', simple models or sets of ideas, by which they make sense of the world. New experiences are assimilated into the schemas. That is, they are understood by reference to existing patterns of thinking. For example, a very young girl may refer to all animals as 'cat'; this would have been the first animal she learned about, and so all future encounters with animals are understood in terms of the schema 'cat'.

Gradually, she comes to realise that there are significant differences between animals and that different words (and schemas) are needed. In this way, the child *accommodates* her learning to the new experience. That is, the new experience cannot be *assimilated* into existing schemas, and so the schemas have to change – accommodation has to take place.

This is very significant in relation to children away from home learning about new experiences. They may attempt, against all the odds, to avoid accommodation (and the painful changes this can entail) and to assimilate the new experience into existing schemas. Growing up can be seen as a process of letting go of more childish or immature schemas and gradually replacing them with more mature ones.

ii. Egocentricity

This is a term which means, quite literally, 'self-centredness'. However, it is not quite the same as selfishness. Young children are said to go through an 'egocentric' phase in the very early stages of life, as they have not yet learned to see the world in a wider context; it is as if everything revolves around them.

It is often argued that adolescence is also a period of egocentricity. Teenagers can become withdrawn and self-centred as they pass from childhood to adulthood or, indeed, they can be brash and self-centred. These would be seen as different aspects of the same underlying issue – the egocentricity of adolescence. One way in which this can manifest itself is through acute self-consciousness. Teenagers can feel that everyone is watching them or even persecuting them, hence the common refrain of 'Everyone's picking on me'.

These are just two aspects of Piaget's theory of cognitive development. There are many more that we have not touched on here but which merit further attention. Similarly, there are other theoretical approaches which offer further insights into the way patterns of thinking develop in children and young people. It is a vast area of study and one you will be able to learn about more on a gradual basis through further reading, discussion and practical experience.

Cognitive development is often referred to as 'psychological' development, but this is misleading, as it takes no account of the other key dimension of psychological development – the emotional. Cognitive and emotional development are both important parts of psychological development, and so it is to the emotional issues that we now turn.

2. The emotional strand

Probably the most influential theory of emotional development is what is known as 'attachment theory' and usually associated with the work of John Bowlby. The basic idea underlying the theory is that young children need to form a close maternal bond. Pithers (1987, p. 2) quotes from Bowlby's classic work *Maternal Care and Mental Health*:

> What is believed to be essential for mental health is that the infant and young child should experience a warm, intimate and continuous relationship with his mother (or permanent mother-substitute) in which both find satisfaction and enjoyment.

Bowlby is using the term 'mental health' in the sense of healthy emotional development. He argued that children who do not have the benefit of this bond of warmth and affection are likely to become 'affectionless thieves' – manipulative and calculating people who are unable to show affection.

Pithers comments:

> We all know children who having been denied warm experiences in early life, have become emotional calculators, incapable of spontaneous response, insensible to the feelings of others, demanding and insistent, often turning other people into their service without return. That this arises through early relationships is seldom doubted. (ibid.)

This has been an extremely influential theory, although it has also been heavily criticised, particularly in terms of the way it reinforces stereotypical gender roles by focusing on mothering rather than parenting (see Howe, 1995, for a more up-to-date perspective). Bowlby's emphasis on the mother's role in successful emotional development has become known as the 'maternal deprivation thesis'. This notion was a major influence in the movement away from residential care for young children to fostering, where 'substitute' mothering could take place.

One of the key aspects of Bowlby's theory is the concept of loss. He argued that children who do not have satisfactory maternal bonding will grieve for the loss they experience. This concept of loss is an important one and we shall return to it below when we explore crisis theory.

There are, of course, many other aspects of emotional development in addition to the role of bonding. These include self-image and self-esteem (to be discussed in Chapter 3), emotional abuse (to be discussed in Chapter 5) and the various methods of coping with emotions such as anger, pain, embarrassment and so on.

Coping with such feelings is traditionally seen as a progression from a set of very 'childish' responses to a more 'mature' set. However, this is a good example of the dangers of adopting a simple, biologically based stage model of development. Stages can be identified, but these need to be linked to other factors rather than simply to 'biological maturation'. For example, what is considered childish in one culture may be regarded as mature in others. Similarly, there are class differences in terms of what is seen as an acceptable emotional response – for example, the English 'stiff upper lip' tends to be associated more with the upper classes. Equally, there are distinct gender differences in terms of what we see as an appropriate emotional response – consider the notion that 'big boys don't cry'.

In trying to understand emotional development, we must remember to relate these emotional issues to the wider social context in which they arise. It is important to see emotions as ways of dealing with aspects of the outside world and adjusting to the impact they have on us. They reflect the relationship between personal, subjective factors such as values, beliefs and interests, and external circumstances, events and so on. If the two sets of factors are in conflict, negative emotions such as fear, anxiety or anger will be felt. If, however, the two are in harmony, positive emotions such as joy and hope will result. Figure 2.5 helps to clarify this.

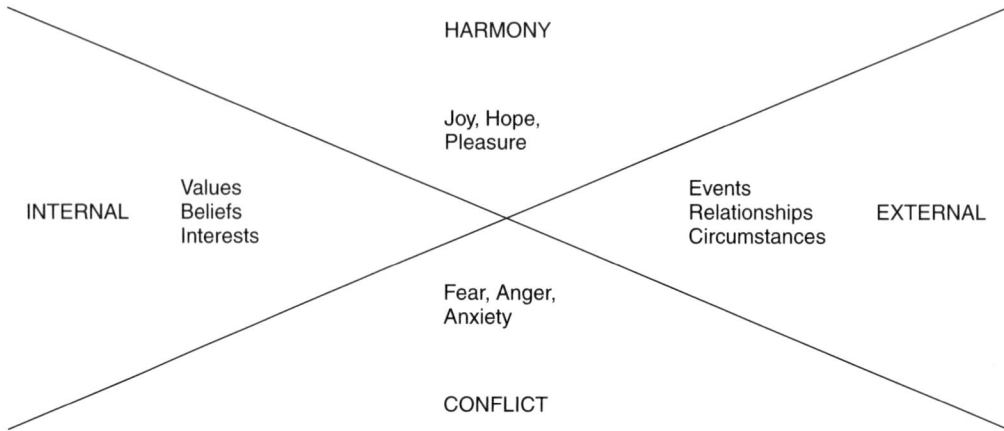

Figure 2.5   Emotion as a response to the external world

Emotions can therefore be seen as part of our relationship with the world – and again we can see that the social divisions of class, race, gender, disability and so on are significant parts of that world. What this means is that there can be no simple, clear-cut model of emotional development, no formula to follow in order to understand children's emotional needs and problems. It is therefore more helpful to think in terms of a framework for understanding how and why emotional problems arise. Developing this framework will be part of the remaining two sections of this chapter.

Emotional development is a complex area, and so it may be helpful to spend a little time reflecting on the issues before moving on to consider the social strand of development. Exercise 2.2 is designed to help you with this.

Exercise 2.2

The first stage of this exercise is to 'brainstorm' a list of emotions. Take a separate piece of paper and write down as many emotions as you can think of.

The second stage is to consider each of these emotions in terms of: In what ways do they serve a useful purpose? In what ways can they be a barrier to progress? How do you recognise particular emotions? Is it possible for different emotions to manifest themselves in similar or identical ways? Use these questions (and any other which occur to you) as the basis of a discussion with your colleagues.

---

3. *The social strand*

Social development is traditionally given far less attention than the other aspects of development outlined so far. It is, none the less, a crucial dimension of how children grow and develop. The area covered by this term is a very broad one, and so it is helpful to divide it up into its component parts. These are illustrated in Figure 2.6 (opposite).

Moral development is the process by which children learn to distinguish between right and wrong and to understand what is acceptable or unacceptable within their culture. This development is brought about by a number of processes such as approval and encouragement, on the one hand, and disapproval, discipline and punishment, on the other. There are also certain rituals or cultural patterns which are used to make sure, as far as possible, that children learn the moral values of their culture. This is a key part of the process known as 'socialisation'.

MORAL	INTERPERSONAL
learning right from wrong; transmission of cultural norms and values	relating to others; social skills; behaviour
SOCIAL LOCATION	POLITICAL
class; race and culture; gender; age; disability and so on	power; rights; freedom from abuse

Figure 2.6   The main components of social development

A common mistake in trying to understand moral development is to see unacceptable behaviour in children as either a sign that they are 'bad', 'wicked' or 'evil' children, or that they have not been properly socialised. To see children as inherently 'bad' is a problem in two ways. First, it ignores the major role of socialisation and the strong influence of society and culture on our development. Second, it writes children off, dismisses them as beyond help and is therefore potentially very oppressive.

To see unacceptable behaviour as simply the result of inadequate socialisation is to ignore the significance of other factors, including:

- value conflict: some behaviour is based on socialisation to different or conflicting values (for example, different class values) rather than a *lack* of socialisation;
- peer group pressure: children will often behave in ways that go against their better judgement as a result of the influences of other children; and
- emotional stress: children's behaviour is often based not on rational, moral principles, but rather on emotional pressures, turmoil or unmet needs.

Interpersonal development includes learning about relationships, about social skills and about 'age-appropriate' behaviour. Children need to learn the 'rules' of forming relationships which operate in their particular society and culture. Some children learn these rules very quickly, but others may take longer or may need advice or coaching.

Children also need to develop social skills. This includes relationship building, but also goes far beyond this to cover such matters as: manners and social customs; appropriate terms of address or ways of engaging in conversation; power relations and patterns of deference or respect.

It is also necessary for children to learn about social expectations in relation to what behaviour is seen as appropriate according to the age of the child. That is, we tend to see some behaviours as acceptable for children of a certain age but not acceptable for other children of a different age. For example, a young child singing in a public place may be seen as charming, whereas a sixteen-year old doing so is likely to be seen as a nuisance.

Social location is also a key part of social development. This involves children learning where they fit into society in terms of social divisions such as class, race and gender. Again, this is a major feature of socialisation. Take, for example, gender. Society has very strong expectations of how boys should think, feel and act and how girls should. Gender roles are often clearly demarcated and 'transgressions' can be punished by, for example, ridicule and disapproval. Where boys do not fit in with an image of masculinity, they can be labelled 'cissy' or 'effeminate'. Where girls do not live up to a feminine image, they are seen as 'butch' or 'tomboys'. This is a very sensitive area of social development and carries with it considerable scope for oppression and discrimination.

The political dimension of social development is one which is receiving increasing attention. Politics is about power, and so the important issues here are the amount of power and influence children are allowed to have and it is about their rights. In short, it is about how much of a voice children are allowed to have. This is an issue which has gained in significance with the implementation of the Children Act 1989. It is also very relevant to anti-discriminatory practice with its focus on empowerment. This is one of the reasons why partnership, with its emphasis on involving children, is such an important concept. It is one to which we shall return in Chapter 3.

From the preceding pages we can see that there are many sides to child development and no simple solution to the problems of understanding how children develop or how development goes wrong. However, we have laid the foundations for continued learning on this topic as it is such a central issue for working with children and young people in an informed way.

To conclude this section on child development, it is worth reproducing what Branthwaite and Rogers (1985, p. 57) see as three fundamental principles of child development:

1. Abilities evolve out of experience and are tuned to the child's needs to handle particular environments. This is an active process on the child's part to discover the properties of things, make events predictable and control what happens.
2. Children's understanding of the world around them differs from that of adults. Development involves the correct identification of different kinds of problem and the ability to apply an appropriate strategy for solving that problem.
3. Development proceeds by progressive differentiation of experience; and the evolution of more complex skills proceeds by adapting and integrating simpler, well-rehearsed abilities.

Exercise 2.3

Consider the three principles outlined above. Try to think of a concrete example of each of the three. Make some notes about this.

NB This exercise is more difficult than it sounds at first. If you get stuck, compare notes with a colleague or your line manager and tackle the problem together.

Identity formation

As we grow and develop, we form a sense of self or personal identity. This is not something which is fixed or predetermined, as the identity which emerges owes a great deal to a range of psychological and social factors which influence us. This section will outline some of the main factors in identity formation and some of the ways in which the process can be problematic.

The first stage in developing a sense of self is a very basic one, as the following passage from Branthwaite (1985) indicates:

> In children, the idea of self as a separate and distinct person is only gradually acquired through development. Very young children do not differentiate themselves from the environment, and they probably are not aware of a clear boundary between their own bodies and their physical

surroundings. The child only gradually learns to distinguish self from the inanimate environment and other people. (p. 34)

Gradually, each of us develops a sense of self, an identify which acts as the basis of our experience of the world. The process of identity formation is a very complex one and much has been written on the subject. There is considerable debate and disagreement about many aspects but, for present purposes, we shall be adopting an approach to the subject based on the following assumptions or premises:

1. Identity is dynamic. That is, it will be subject to change and modification over time;
2. Identity consists of two main elements – *self-image* (how we see ourselves) and *self-esteem* (how we value ourselves);
3. Identity has social roots. That is, who we are depends very much on where we are in society.

Let us now look at each of these three areas in turn to see what light they cast on group care with children and young people. To say that identity is dynamic is, in fact, a statement which brings hope. Traditional views which see identity as something which never changes give no hope to people whose sense of self is, in some way, problematic. This is particularly significant in relation to children, for to adopt a non-dynamic view is to see change as impossible. This amounts to writing children off. We need to resist the temptation of saying 'He'll never change' or 'She can't help it, it's her nature'. People can, and do, change and this is especially true of children. Change may be difficult and complex, but this is not the same as saying that it is not feasible. Arguing that change is not possible can actually make it impossible – it becomes a 'self-fulfilling prophecy'. That is, if we deny the possibility of change, we are, in fact, closing the door on such a possibility. Changes in our sense of self usually take place gradually and are linked to changes in our self-image and/or level of self-esteem.

Self-image has been explained in terms of what Cooley (1902) calls 'the looking-glass self'. That is, how I see myself mirrors or reflects how other people see me. I receive feedback from others and interpret this in the light of my self-image. This, then, becomes a two-way process. How I see myself depends on how others see me (I am influenced by their perceptions of me) but, also, how others see me depends on how I see myself (how I present myself to others). Figure 2.7 should help to clarify how this complex process works.

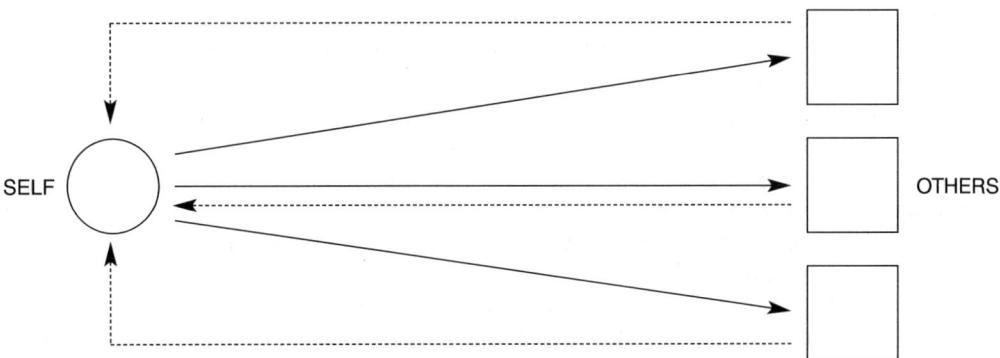

Stage 1: I project an image of myself (⎯⎯⎯➤)

Stage 2: I receive feedback from others (--------➤) some of which reinforces my image, some of which conflicts with it.

Stage 3: I modify accordingly the image I project (and this returns me to stage 2).

Figure 2.7 The 'looking-glass' self

Part of this process is 'labelling'. For example, if a child is labelled as 'thief', this can be very influential in shaping the child's behaviour and attitudes. Once again, it can become a self-fulfilling prophecy and actually encourage criminal behaviour. It is for this reason that we must be very careful not to attach negative or potentially harmful labels to children. Telling a child that he or she is stupid is likely to sap confidence and thereby contribute to lower educational achievement.

These issues are closely linked to the notion of 'self-esteem'. Self-esteem is a term used to describe the extent to which we value ourselves. At one extreme, people with high self-esteem are confident and secure and have faith in themselves. At the other extreme, people with low self-esteem will tend to lack confidence and may be prone to depression or self-destructive behaviours. In view of this, it is important that we do not reinforce negative aspects of children's behaviour or attitudes. We need to concentrate on maximising positives and building on children's strengths. This is an important point and one to which we shall return in Chapter 3.

Unfortunately, significant numbers of children in group care have low self-esteem, no doubt largely as a result of the painful and damaging circumstances of family breakdown, often reinforced and intensified by foster placement breakdowns and so on. The children in our care so often have a painful history of failure and rejection. It is little wonder that they may find trust a difficult commitment to make.

These messages of failure and rejection are, of course, even stronger for children from ethnic minorities who are likely to have the added burden of racism to contend with. They will have been brought up in a society which so often gives the message that 'different equals inferior'. Branthwaite (1985) refers to a research study which showed that: 'black children in Britain, just like their American counterparts, recognise racial differences and have a strong tendency to devalue their own group' (p. 38).

This leads us on to the third aspect of identity: its social roots. As Mead (1964) puts it: 'it is impossible to conceive of a self arising outside of social experience' (p. 204). My consciousness of who I am as an individual is in many ways unique. However, we also have to recognise that our identities are heavily influenced by social factors. Figure 2.8 illustrates some of these main influences.

One of the ways in which these social influences manifest themselves is in terms of 'social roles'. A role is a set of expectations. When a person occupies a certain role (for example, residential child care worker) a number of expectations are associated with that role. There are roles associated with each of the influences outlined in Figure 2.8, and these can be highly significant in terms of identity. Take, for example, gender. Society has, for the most part, clear expectations about what is appropriate 'masculine' behaviour for boys and men and 'feminine' behaviour for girls and women. This can cause a number of problems: girls who assert themselves can be seen as aggressive and 'unfeminine', while boys who experience pain and distress may feel they should not cry or express their emotions. Sticking rigidly to conventional gender roles therefore has oppressive consequences.

Before moving on to consider other aspects of identity formation which can prove problematic, spend a little time tackling Exercise 2.4. It is designed to help you relate some of the theoretical ideas about identity to your own experience.

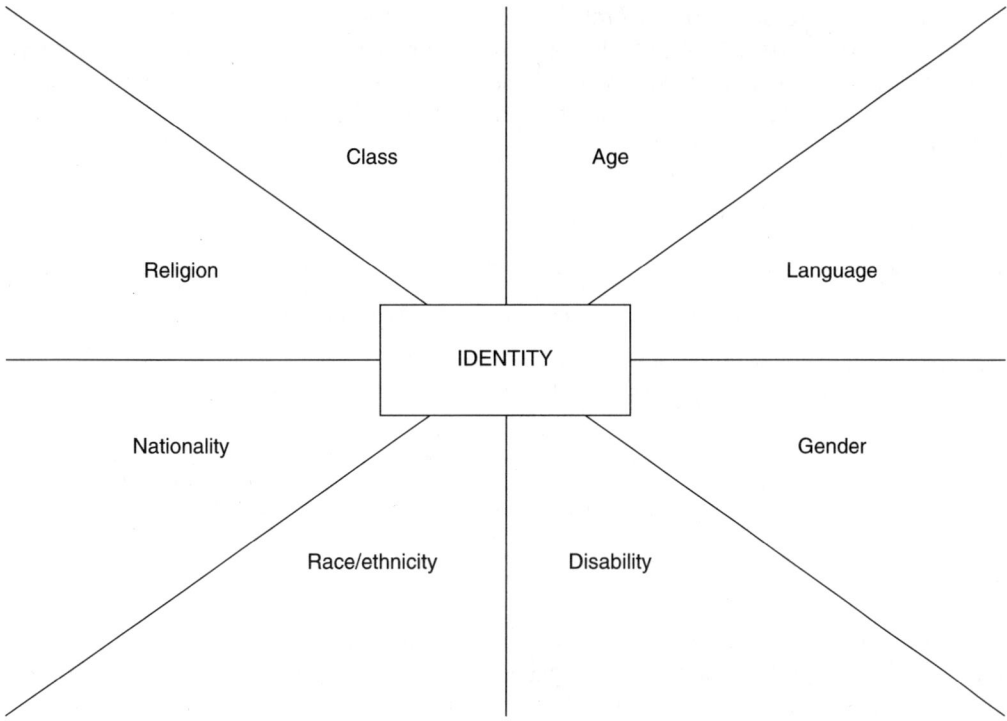

Figure 2.8   Social influences on identity

Exercise 2.4

Think back to your own childhood and consider what were the important factors in the development of your identity. Use your own experience to answer the following questions:

- How would you describe yourself in terms of the eight social influences shown in Figure 2.8? For example, what is your class background, your religion?
- How have these influenced the person you are today? What impact have they had on your identity? Try to think of concrete examples.
- Were there particular people, events or situations which were significant in terms of your self-esteem? What made you feel good and valued? What were the obstacles to feeling good about yourself?

NB Due to the personal nature of this exercise, there may be aspects which you may not wish to discuss with others. This is fine, but do take the opportunity to discuss at least some of the less private issues with colleagues. Identity is an important issue in child care and you and your colleagues can learn a great deal from each other by sharing views.

As we have seen, identity formation is a complex matter with many dimensions. But it is worth wrestling with these complexities as the subject is such an important one for child care. The fact that children have reached a stage where some form of alternative care is necessary implies that circumstances which can hinder or damage identity formation are likely to have arisen. In addition, the circumstances of actually being cared for away from home can also be very harmful – for example, pressure from other children to commit offences or to behave inappropriately.

Identity can therefore be a very problematic area for children and young people in group care. Problems can be unique to particular children but there are also patterns or 'commonalities' which can be recognised. There are also particular approaches or strategies which can be used to try to deal with such problems. Figure 2.9 summarises some of the main problems and possible strategies.

PROBLEM	STRATEGY
Low self-esteem	Focus on positives; give encouragement and praise; set tasks which can easily be achieved – build up confidence gradually; in disapproving of a child's behaviour, make it clear that it is the behaviour that you disapprove of and not the child.
Labelling	Be very wary of attaching negative labels to children even in fun – humour is a powerful source of victimisation; discourage children from attaching labels to each other; encourage positive aspects of the child's identity.
Social disadvantage	Encourage awareness of social issues such as deprivation, racism, sexism. Set ground rules which do not allow discriminatory language or behaviour (for example, racist or sexist). Encourage positive images (for example, of black children).

Figure 2.9   Identity problems and strategies.

The strategies suggested in Figure 2.9 are by no means definitive. They would, however, act as the basis of a group discussion amongst your colleagues so that you could develop your own strategies to suit the children and the circumstances you are dealing with.

Identity problems, and responses to them, are important aspects of assessment. We will therefore return to this subject in Chapter 3 when assessment and planning are the main topics to be addressed.

Coping with stress, change, rejection and loss

Children in general have to learn to cope with some degree of stress, change, rejection and loss. For children in group care the situation is likely to be more extreme. They are likely to have experienced more than their fair share of each, and often without having adequate support systems to fall back on.

Arroba and James (1987) define stress as our response to an inappropriate level of pressure. (We shall have more to say about this in Chapter 8 when we consider the effects of stress upon staff.) Children who have experienced family breakdown, and particularly those who have been abused, may have been subjected to extremes of tension and pressure. It is not surprising, therefore, that such children can react strongly to pressures brought to bear upon them. Many of the behavioural problems displayed by children can be seen as a response to such pressures, especially if the situation raised echoes of other, more painful pressures encountered in the past. It can be helpful to understand such behaviour in this context. This is particularly the case for adolescents who, in some cultures at least, have considerable pressures upon them as a result of their 'transitional' status between childhood and adulthood.

Adolescents are expected to relinquish childish behaviours and adopt a more mature and responsible attitude towards their lives and the people around them. This does not mean to say that adolescence is necessarily a time of what is often referred to as 'storm and stress'. The stereotypical view of the adolescent is of a troubled and troublesome youngster who is very volatile and unpredictable. However, research has shown that this is a stereotype and is certainly not the case for the majority of adolescents (Frosh *et al.*, 2003).

If the children in our care do demonstrate problematic behaviour, we should be wary of putting this down to 'normal' problems of adolescence. We could then very easily dismiss significant underlying problems – for example, unmet needs, excessive pressures or a lack of clear boundaries of acceptable behaviour. Adolescence is a time of change and thus of loss, but most teenagers adjust to the changes without major problems, although some degree of conflict and 'testing out' is not uncommon. However, for the adolescent in group care, it is likely that he or she will have experienced a number of additional changes and losses, many of them negative, painful and destructive. Such changes (of placement, for example) often give a message of failure and rejection and, as we saw above, this can have a significant impact on self-esteem and identity. Even where such changes do not amount to rejection or failure, they are often perceived by the child as such. Low self-esteem becomes a vicious circle as events or situations are interpreted in a negative way, and this then reinforces feelings of worthlessness.

There are many ways of helping children cope with stress, change, rejection and loss (see the 'Guide to further learning' section for details). But, for present purposes, I shall focus on just one example. The technique I have chosen is based on crisis intervention theory (see Thompson, 1991). A crisis is a situation in which our usual ways of coping are no longer applicable. This can sometimes cause us to panic but does not necessarily do so. Once we have begun to get over the shock or initial impact of the crisis, there are a number of ways in which the situation can develop:

1. The person concerned can feel helpless, powerless and paralysed (for example, depression).
2. He or she can panic and act in an inappropriate or destructive way (for example, aggression).
3. The situation can be denied or avoided, often at great cost to the individual concerned (for example, absconding).
4. The person concerned can learn new and better coping skills and methods and can therefore grow and develop as a result of the crisis.

According to crisis intervention theory, the task of the worker is to help the child through the crisis by avoiding 1 to 3 and working very strongly towards 4. This can be done by focusing on the positives of the situation; helping the child learn new, constructive ways of coping; reassuring him or her that this is a process we all go through from time to time (perhaps giving an example from your own experience); being there and showing that you care.

There are three particular aspects of this approach which you should note:

1. A 'crisis' is not just a major drama or emergency. It is a situation where our usual coping tactics prove to be inadequate. Children with a low level of social skills development and/or a background deprived of positive life experiences, are likely to experience many crises in this sense of the word.
2. A crisis generates a lot of emotional energy. This energy can be used positively/constructively or negatively/destructively. The task of crisis intervention is to channel this energy in the positive direction.
3. Crisis intervention is a form of empowerment. It helps children and young people to learn to cope effectively with problems and pressures and thus supports them in taking control of, and responsibility for, their lives and actions.

Exercise 2.5 is intended as a means of helping you understand some of these issues in terms of your work experience. Spend some time now working through the questions in the exercise before moving on to the concluding section.

> **Exercise 2.5**
>
> Think about your recent experiences with the children or young people you work with. Try to remember two or three recent instances of behaviour you found unacceptable, then, once you have these clear in your mind, try to answer the following questions:
>
> 1. Were any of these incidents the result of a child feeling unable to cope with the situation (for example, coping with conflict)? If so, please describe how. If not, can you think of other situations where a child being ill-equipped to cope has led to problems?
> 2. How could you have responded to such a situation in terms of crisis intervention?
> 3. If you were to develop your use of the crisis intervention approach, in which ways would you need help or support (for example, from colleagues or your line manager)?

Conclusion

The main focus in this chapter has been understanding the various dimensions of children's needs. Underpinning this have been three major themes:

1. Children's needs are not standard, uniform or fixed (although a number of commonalities do occur). Need has to be seen in the context of:
   - stage of development – cognitive, emotional and social as well as physical;
   - social circumstances, including class, race and gender;
   - identity formation in general and self-esteem in particular; and
   - responses to stress, change and rejection.
2. Many of the problems encountered by child care workers can be seen to be related to children's unmet needs. These unmet needs can manifest themselves as:
   - aggressive or challenging behaviour;
   - withdrawal, depression and a lack of co-operation; and
   - self-destructive behaviours such as drug misuse, self-inflicted injuries or even suicide attempts.
3. The fact that the children we deal with are in group care means that it is quite likely that they will have had a number of painful, distressing and destructive experiences. Any attempt to understand their needs without taking these factors into account is therefore going to be, at best, superficial, and, at worst, disastrous.

Having thus explored some of the key aspects of the complex area of understanding children's needs, it is time to move on to examine some of the issues which apply to the process of assessing those needs. A framework for assessment is a central part of care planning for children. Assessment is a major feature of Chapter 3, which addresses the area of care planning. The discussions in the next part therefore build on the issues studied here.

Guide to further learning

1. Theories of need

Berry. J. (1972) *Social Work with Children*, London, RKP.
Kellmer Pringle, M. (1986) *The Needs of Children*, 3rd edn, London, Hutchinson.

2. Child development

General

Davenport, G.C. (1994) *An Introduction to Child Development*, 2nd edn, London, Collins.

Oates, J. (1994) *The Foundations of Child Development*, Oxford, Basil Blackwell.

Thompson, N. (2002) *Building the Future: Social Work with Children, Young People and Their Families,* Chapter 1.

Stage models of development

Erikson, E.M. (1977) *Childhood and Society*, London, Paladin.

Fahlberg, F. (1982) *Child Development*, London, BAAF.

Cognitive development

Piaget, J. (1958) *The Child's Construction of Reality*, London, Routledge and Kegan Paul.

Piaget, J. and Inhelder, B. (1958) *The Growth of Logical Thinking. From Childhood to Adolescence*, London, Routledge and Kegan Paul.

Piaget, J. and Inhelder, B. (1964) *The Early Growth of Logic in the Child*, London, Routledge and Kegan Paul.

Emotional development

Axline, V. (1971) *Dibs: In Search of Self*, Harmondsworth, Penguin.

Barnes, P. (1995) *Personal, Social and Emotional Development of Children*, Oxford, Basil Blackwell.

Daniel, B., Wassell, S. and Gilligan, R. (1999) *Child Development for Child Care and Protection Workers*, London, Jessica Kingsley Publishers.

Howe, D. (1995) *Attachment Theory for Social Work Practice*, Basingstoke, Macmillan – now Palgrave Macmillan.

Stevens, R. (1983) *Freud and Psychoanalysis*, Milton Keynes, Open University Press.

Social development

Barnes, P (1995) *Personal, Social and Emotional Development of Children*, Oxford, Basil Blackwell.

Holt, J. (1964) *How Children Fail*, Harmondsworth, Penguin.

Identity formation

Coleman, C. and Hendry, L. (1990) *The Nature of Adolescence*, 2nd edn, London, Routledge.

Erikson, E. (1968) *Identity, Youth and Crisis*, London, Faber.

Goffman, E. (1968) *Stigma: Notes on the Management of Spoiled Identity*, Harmondsworth, Penguin.

Mead, G.H. (1934) *Mind, Self and Society*, University of Chicago Press.

Wheal, A. (1998) *Adolescence: Positive Approaches for Working with Young People*, Lyme Regis, Russell House Publishing.

Coping with stress, change, rejection and loss

Butler, I. and Williamson, H. (1994) *Children Speak: Children, Trauma and Social Work*, Harlow, Longman.

Kroll, B. (1994) *Chasing Rainbows: Children, Divorce and Loss*, Lyme Regis, Russell House Publishing.

Rutter, M. (1975) *Helping Troubled Children*, Harmondsworth, Penguin.

Thompson, N. (ed.) (2002) *Loss and Grief: A Guide for Human Services Practitioners*, Basingstoke, Palgrave Macmillan.

Chapter 3

Care Planning

Introduction

The issue of planning is a central one in the distinction between good and bad child care practice. An absence of planning is strongly associated with poor practice and a poorly thought-out approach to meeting children's needs.

In a way, planning is simply a reflection of one aspect of good parenting – being aware of the changing needs of children as they grow and develop and preparing to take the necessary steps to meet them. However, for group care workers, it is also more complex than this in two ways:

1. For the majority of parenting situations, the overall, long-term plan is straightforward – to remain in the care of one's parents until maturity and independence. The long-term future of children in group care is often not so clear cut.
2. Professional workers have to be more systematic and explicit in their planning to ensure that the situation does not drift by losing direction or impetus – a real danger when a number of people share responsibility for planning.

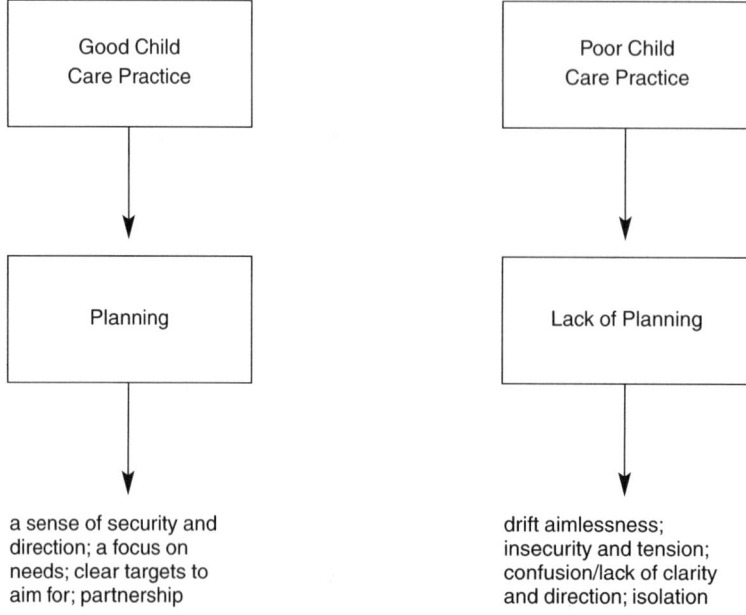

Good Child Care Practice	Poor Child Care Practice
↓	↓
Planning	Lack of Planning
↓	↓
a sense of security and direction; a focus on needs; clear targets to aim for; partnership	drift aimlessness; insecurity and tension; confusion/lack of clarity and direction; isolation

Figure 3.1   The importance of care planning

The value and importance of care planning have long been understood and appreciated but, unfortunately, this has not always ensured that the planning process has been given the time and attention it needs if it is to be effective. The aim in this chapter, therefore, is to give you some of the basic tools you need for care planning, to give you a framework and a set of ideas to help you develop a systematic and constructive approach. It cannot provide you with the skills and competencies necessary, but it can give you a foundation on which to build.

Cast your mind back to the discussion of the Kolb learning cycle in the Introduction. It is very relevant here. Reading this chapter will provide you with a concrete experience, and this will need to be followed up by reflection (thinking about the issues raised), conceptualisation (relating the new ideas, and your own thoughts about them, to your previous learning) and experimentation (trying the ideas out in practice). But, it is also important that you should not see this as a solitary activity. Once again, you need to remember that you have much to learn from your colleagues and they can learn from you – so do engage in discussion with them and share ideas together.

Exercise 3.1

Re-read the section of the Introduction that outlines the Kolb Learning Cycle to refresh your memory of how it works. Once you have done this, think about something you have learned from this book so far and see if you can relate your learning process to the learning cycle. Did you go through the cycle? Can you identify the steps?

When you've done this, check out with your colleagues what their experiences of the learning cycle have been.

The remainder of this chapter is devoted to two key aspects of care planning. First, I shall address issues of assessment and consider what the major components of this are. Second, I shall explore the notion of partnership and clarify how and why it has a major role to play in the process of care planning.

Assessment

One of the criticisms of assessment in the past is that it has been too narrow and too negative. It has been too narrow by focusing too closely on the child without paying adequate attention to the network of contextual factors which make up the environment in which the child lives and has lived. This echoes Aldgate's (1988) call for an 'ecological' approach: 'that is, an approach based on the interaction between human beings and their environment' (p. 5).

Assessment has often been too negative by concentrating too heavily on the child's problems (or, worse still, the problems the child causes rather than the ones he or she experiences). One particularly worrying aspect of this is the use of the term 'problem child': As Herbert (1985) points out, the term 'problem child' is an oversimplification: it makes it sound as though the problem belongs to the child alone, whereas it may be the 'problem situation' which needs attention (Adcock *et al.*, 1989, p. 204).

Indeed, the assessment needs to be much wider than just the child him- or herself and needs to highlight the positives and strengths of the situation as well as the negatives and weaknesses.

What is needed is a more systematic approach to assessment – a clear and constructive process which enables the formulation of clear and helpful plans. The next section provides an outline of one such systematic approach.

Process and framework

There is no single, definitive approach to assessment, although the process and framework outlined here will stand you in good stead in developing a systematic approach to assessment. The process consists of five main stages which act in a cyclical way. That is, once we reach Stage 5, we commence a new cycle of assessment and find ourselves at a new Stage 1. That is, assessment is continuous and ongoing and is not a one-off event. Figure 3.2 represents the cyclical process we shall be using as our basic framework.

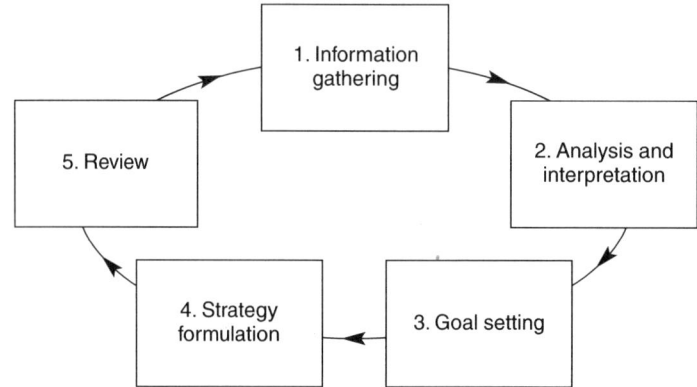

Figure 3.2   The process of assessment

We shall look at each of these five areas in turn.

Assessment needs to be based on relevant and accurate information concerning various aspects of the child's or young person's life and circumstances:

- personal characteristics, interests, wishes and feelings;
- health needs and background history;
- family composition and social circumstances (finance, housing and so on);
- ethnic and cultural background, religious beliefs and practices;
- educational history;
- factors leading to current situation; response and attitude to these factors;
- behaviour and social skills;
- relationships with peers and adults;
- and so on.

1. *Information gathering*

It is not simply a matter of gathering as much information as possible. If it were, we could easily get bogged down in a mass of detail. The guiding principle should be to gather information which is relevant to care planning – information which has a bearing on significant issues from the past as well as present circumstances and future wishes and intentions. It is also important to remember that information gathering should actively involve the child or young person concerned. His or her involvement should help to ensure that the information is consistent with his or her experience.

2. *Analysis and interpretation*

Information only has value if it helps us to understand the person or situation concerned. For this to happen we need to have a framework with which to make sense of it. That is, we need to analyse and interpret the information to see what patterns emerge.

One useful framework for doing this is what is known as SWOT analysis. This entails outlining the Strengths, Weaknesses, Opportunities and Threats which apply to the child and his or her circumstances (see Figure 3.3). The value of this approach is that it does not concentrate simply on problems but also adopts a more positive approach by considering the strengths and opportunities which apply.

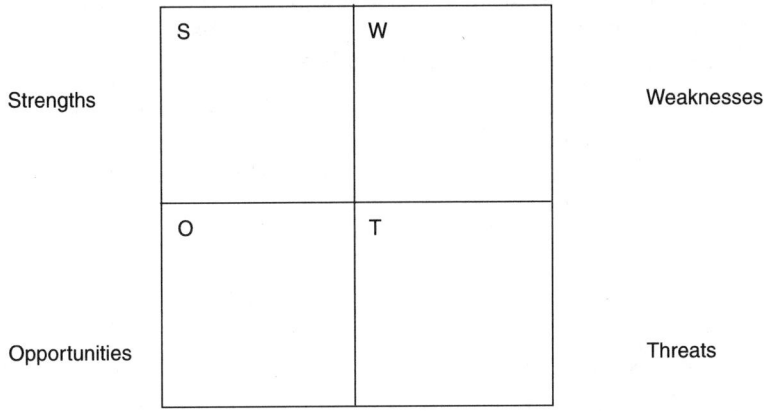

Figure 3.3   SWOT analysis

This framework can usefully be used directly with the child or young person concerned to identify each of the four areas. One particular advantage of using the framework in this way is that it will often emerge that some things are seen as both a strength and a weakness, or both a threat and an opportunity (or other such combination). Which side will dominate, positive or negative, will depend to a large extent on the care planning process and how successfully it is implemented.

Exercise 3.2

Spend a little time considering your own personal circumstances at the moment. Can you identify particular strengths, weaknesses, opportunities and threats? Take a sheet of paper, reproduce Figure 3.3 on it and then use the diagram to make notes under the appropriate headings.

Are there any issues which fit in one or more boxes? If so, what implications does this have for how you should deal with them?

---

3. *Goal setting*

The term 'goal' is used to refer to what we are aiming for, what we are trying to achieve. It is very important that we are clear about what our goals are, for the following reasons:

- Being clear about what we are aiming for motivates us to achieve these goals by giving a sense of purpose and direction.

- It helps people working together to pull in the same direction, and therefore promotes partnership.
- It gives a clear and consistent message to the child or young person concerned.
- It gives us a baseline from which to measure progress and evaluate the effectiveness of our actions.

Goals can be seen to operate at two different, but related, levels. These are:

Aims: Aims tend to be broad, and wide-ranging, for example: 'To reunite Tony with his family'. *Objectives*: These tend to be more specific and may be more difficult to define or determine. They are the component parts of the broader aim, for example: 'To improve relationships between Tony and his parents to the point where they can live in relative harmony together'. Achieving the specific objective of improving relationships between Tony and his family contributes to the broader overall aim of reuniting Tony with his family.

It is helpful if objectives are phrased in such a way as to be measurable. However, this may not always be possible without making them very contrived. Characteristically, the two levels (aims and objectives) exist in a 'cascade' relationship. That is, one aim produces a number of objectives. This is illustrated in Figure 3.4.

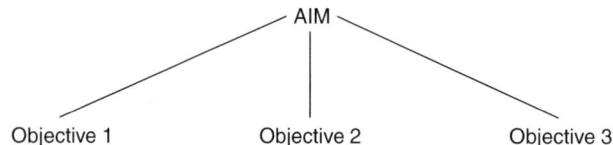

Figure 3.4   The cascade of aims and objectives

4. *Strategy formulation*

Once we have completed goal setting, we have established where we want to be. The next question is: How do we get there? This is the stage of strategy formulation. Our strategy is the route we follow in order to try and meet our objectives. It is a process of identifying:

- what needs to change;
- what needs to be maintained/safeguarded;
- how these objectives are to be met;
- who is responsible for what; and
- the date and process of review.

This stage is therefore closely related to Stage 3, goal setting. Formulating a strategy involves translating aims into objectives. However, it is not simply a mechanical process. It is often the case that complexities identified at the strategy formulation stage make it necessary to reconsider the aims and objectives previously agreed. We can then get a 'loop' between Stages 3 and 4, as Figure 3.5 shows.

5. *Review*

Achieving an agreed strategy is a vitally important part of care planning. However, this is by no means the end of the process. Plans can easily be overtaken by events or can prove to have been drawn up on the basis of an error of judgement or inaccurate information. It is therefore important to keep plans under constant review. In particular, it is necessary to confirm a formal process for review. This needs to take account of a number of factors:

- statutory requirements (for example, under the Children Act 1989 or other relevant piece of law);

- identifying what situations would necessitate calling a formal review meeting earlier than planned – for example, the return to the family home of a Schedule I offender (that is, someone who has been convicted of an offence against one or more children);
- who has responsibility for monitoring the situation and activating the formal review process if necessary.

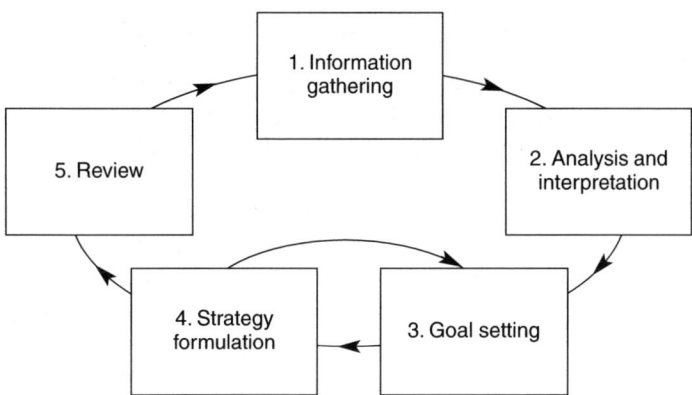

Figure 3.5   Goal setting and strategy formulation

As was emphasised in Chapter 2, children's needs are fluid and dependent on circumstances. In making plans for meeting these needs it is therefore necessary to be flexible and responsive. A well-worked out process of review is a vital part of achieving good practice in this area of child care.

Reviewing takes place at two levels, formal and informal. The formal level relates to review meetings, written reports and so on, as required by the Children Act 1989. The informal level relates to the day-to-day monitoring of progress towards the agreed goals. Review, in this sense, is an ongoing process, rather than a one-off event at specified intervals. It is important to see review in these terms in order to avoid the very real danger of losing sight of the care plans. It is very easy for care plans to be set up at a formal meeting but not actually made into reality at a practical level – the theory remains divorced from the practice.

Anti-discriminatory practice

Establishing a process and framework for assessment takes us some considerable way towards achieving good practice in this aspect of our work. However, these tools will be of far less value if one very significant aspect is missing, that of anti-discriminatory practice. As was emphasised in Chapter 1, good practice must be anti-discriminatory practice. That is, we must take account of factors such as race, gender, disability and so on, and the oppression and discrimination associated with them. Assessment is no exception to this and so, at every stage of the assessment process, we need to keep coming back to the basic important questions of racial and cultural background, gender and disability, and how these:

- have had an impact on past circumstances;
- play a part in the current situation; and
- are likely to influence future plans and their implementation.

Exercise 3.3

In Chapter 1 you were given a number of suggested 'Guidelines for action' in respect of developing anti-discriminatory practice. Your task in this exercise is to re-read those guidelines and to consider how you would apply them to the process of assessment. You might find it helpful to relate the guidelines to particular individuals you have worked with.

These issues apply at each of the five stages of the assessment cycle: information gathering, analysis and interpretation, goal setting, strategy formulation and review. Forgetting to take account of such issues at any stage of the process could render the assessment invalid or, at worst, contribute further to discrimination and oppression.

Good child care depends on good care planning which, in turn, depends on effective assessment. Like most activities, assessment improves with experience and practice – skills are developed and consolidated. For example, in terms of what constitutes relevant information, there is no hard and fast rule, although skills based on experience will help to sharpen up the distinction between relevant and non-relevant information.

My aim here has been to give you a framework of ideas which will help you to develop the skills needed for effective assessment. It is to be hoped that the ideas presented will help to stand you in good stead for the difficult and complex task of deciding how best to help the children and young people you work with. What should also be of help is a consideration of the concept of partnership and how this plays a central role in care planning. It is to this that we now turn.

Partnership

This is a concept which, in recent years, has become increasingly recognised as a central part of good child care practice. It is a notion that is fundamental to the ethos and philosophy of the Children Act 1989. However, even prior to this, the value of people working together to achieve the same aims was recognised by many practitioners and policy makers. But, what exactly do we mean by partnership? Partnership with whom? What does it consist of? Why is it so important? These are some of the many questions often raised and, indeed, these are the issues to be tackled here.

Tunnard (1991) helps us to understand what is meant by partnership:

> A key feature of the Children Act 1989 is its emphasis on partnership. This nice-sounding term makes us feel good, perhaps even to the extent of being offered as a solution to all child-care difficulties. So what does partnership mean, in theory and practice?
>
> The essence of partnership is sharing. It is marked by respect for one another, role divisions, rights to information, accountability, competence and value accorded to individual input. In short, each partner is seen as having something to contribute, power is shared, decisions are made jointly, and roles are not only respected but are also backed by legal and moral rights. (p. 1)

This is a very important passage which highlights a number of key components of partnership. It is worth looking briefly at each of these in turn:

Sharing: A fundamental element of partnership is working together and this necessarily involves sharing (information, power, resources).

Respect for one another: Relationships based on mistrust and a lack of respect are not likely to promote a spirit of co-operation and partnership.

Role divisions: It is helpful to have a division of labour and be clear about who is responsible for what.

Rights to information: Partnership works best when information is shared, with no secrets or hidden agendas.

Accountability: Partnership is based on shared responsibility and so it is important that individuals are accountable for their actions.

Competence: Each member of the partnership has something constructive to offer in terms of knowledge or skills or commitment and so on.

Value accorded to individual input: The contribution of each member needs to be valued if a genuine partnership is to develop.

Power sharing: The aim is to avoid the situation where an individual or 'subgroup' holds more than their fair share of power.

Joint decision making: It is the responsibility of the whole group to reach a decision together as far as possible.

Roles are respected and backed by legal and moral rights: Partnership is based on the legal rights and principles of the Children Act 1989 and the moral rights of children and their carers.

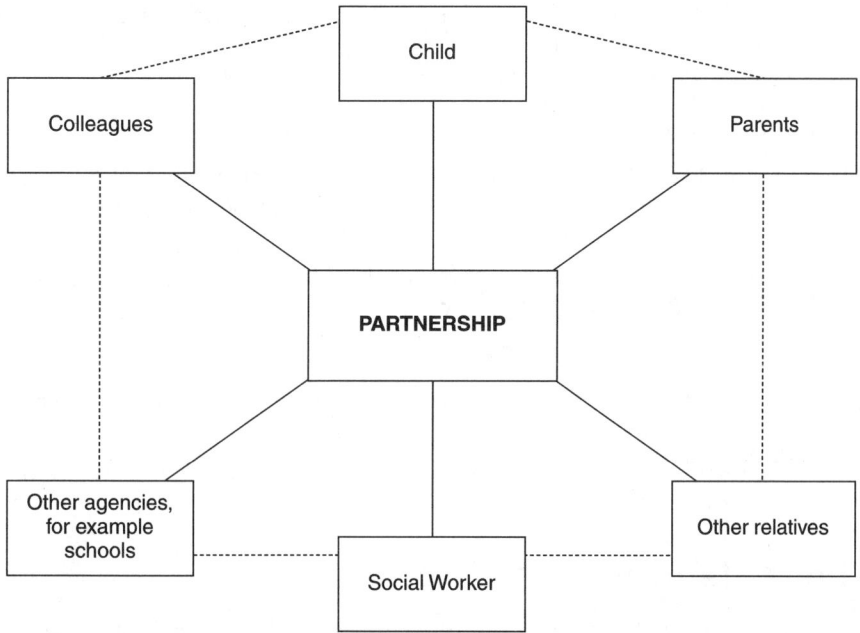

Figure 3.6 Partnership links

Partnership involves a joint effort to solve problems, resolve conflicts and develop a plan for meeting identified needs. As such, it involves a wide range of people, each with a part to play in the care planning process. Figure 3.6 shows the range of possible participants in a partnership. Each of the links within a partnership is potentially vulnerable and can lead to the system breaking down. We therefore need to consider what are the skills required to build firm foundations for partnership.

Building partnerships

Partnership is not a simple matter. It requires skill as well as commitment. But what are these skills? What needs to happen to make partnership work? Perhaps the most effective way of tackling these issues is to consider examples, from our own experience, of partnership situations which have worked well and those which have not worked so well. Exercise 3.4 is designed to help you work through this. Spend some time answering the questions in the exercise and use these to develop your thinking on the subject of partnership. This is a fuller exercise than the ones you've encountered previously so please do resist the temptation to skim quickly through it.

It is hoped that this extended exercise (3.4) will enable you to identify positive steps towards partnership and benefits of striving for success in this area as well as the pitfalls and problems encountered when partnership fails. This will not give you all the information you need, but it will give you foundations on which to build.

Exercise 3.4

Part One   Think about situations you have been involved in at some time in your life which have entailed being in partnership with one or more people. Choose one which seemed to work particularly well and then consider the following questions:

- What was it about the situation which made it a successful partnership? What factors contributed to this?
- What skills did people use which were constructive and effective (for example, communication skills)?
- What benefits did people gain from successful partnership?

Part Two   Think about another partnership situation you have been involved in at some stage of your life. This time choose a situation which did not work well, perhaps one which was a bit of a disaster. Once you have this clear in your mind, consider the following questions:

- What was it about this situation which led to failure?
- What factors contributed to this?

The next step for you is to use partnership as a means of learning. You now have the opportunity of building on your learning by involving your colleagues in discussion. You could also talk to the children and young people that you work with to find out what partnership means to them, how and why it is important and so on.

The benefits of partnership

Before concluding this section it is worthwhile to recap on why partnership is important and what benefits it brings. We can do this by looking briefly at each of the partners. Figure 3.7 conveys some of this information in diagram form.

Perhaps the biggest advantage of partnership is that people feel involved and therefore valued. People are less likely to sabotage or resist plans that they have played a part in formulating. By contrast, plans which are imposed on people with little or no consultation are most prone to resistance and therefore the most vulnerable to failure.

It is also important to remember that a further significant benefit of partnership is that both successes and failures can be shared together. It is a great pleasure to share success as part of a 'team' and it is a great comfort to share failure without feeling isolated or unsupported.

It is clear, therefore, that working in partnership has a number of significant benefits. However, to be realistic, we also need to acknowledge that it can be a difficult aim to achieve and there are often major barriers to achieving a successful partnership. None the less, this chapter has hopefully shown that partnership is a valuable notion and one worthy of the not inconsiderable investment required to make it a reality.

CHILD OR YOUNG PERSON
Does not receive conflicting messages or does not get pulled in different directions; is actively involved in planning and is therefore more committed to making it work.

PARENTS
Less inclined to see the professionals as 'enemies'; enabled to participate as fully as possible and gain confidence from the support of others; more committed to plans they have contributed to.

OTHER RELATIVES
More willing to provide support if they feel they belong; greater opportunity for resolving family tensions and conflicts.

YOU AND COLLEAGUES
Support and co-operation; a clearer picture of what is expected of you and the part you play; the opportunity to tackle conflicts and misunderstandings; shared responsibility.

SOCIAL WORKER
A network of people working together; shared responsibility for developing and implementing care plans; clearer channels for communication; clearer role expectations.

OTHER AGENCIES
An opportunity to contribute knowledge and expertise; a forum for resolving difficulties; a sense of common ownership/commitment.

Figure 3.7: The benefits of partnership

Conclusion

This chapter has sought to emphasise the importance of planning in group care with children and young people and, in particular, the crucial role of the two key concepts of assessment and partnership. Without effective planning there is a tendency to drift; to lose motivation and direction, thereby creating frustration and/or apathy. Planning must therefore occupy a central role in group care (and indeed in all forms of child care).

In order to achieve effective planning, we must have a sound assessment of the circumstances, needs and wishes of the child or young person. To assist you in this we have presented a framework for assessment. In time you may develop a better system of your own or you may modify this system to suit your own requirements. The point remains, however, that it is essential to adopt a systematic approach. A hit and miss approach to assessment is, at best, dangerous and, at worst, a recipe for disaster.

But assessment must be a shared process; it must involve a range of people, not least the children or young people themselves, in sharing information and developing a constructive way forward. In short, it must be based on *partnership*.

The processes of care planning, assessment and building partnerships are seen as an essential part of meeting the needs identified in Chapter 2 in relation to child development, self-esteem and coping with stress, change and rejection. In this way the discussions in Chapter 3 have been built on the issues addressed in Chapter 2. In much the same way, Chapter 3 has 'set the scene' for Chapter 4.

If we are to succeed in developing clear and realistic plans based on sound assessment and partnership, it is important that we are able to communicate well. The processes we have outlined here will falter if the staff involved have difficulties in communicating effectively. It is therefore very appropriate that Chapter 4 addresses the very important area of communication skills. Consequently, we shall now move on to explore what is involved in good communication and what are the pitfalls or barriers which can halt our progress.

Guide to further learning

Care planning: general

Dept of Health (1991) *Patterns and Outcomes in Child Placement*, London, HMSO.

Thompson, N. (2002) *People Skills*, 2nd edn, Basingstoke, Palgrave Macmillan. Chapters 18, 20 and 22.

Assessment

Dwivedi, K.N. (ed,) (2002) *Meeting the Needs of Ethnic Minority Children: A Handbook for Professionals*, London, 2nd edn, London, Jessica Kingsley Publishers.

Horwath, J. (2001) *The Child's World: Assessing Children in Need*, London, Jessica Kingsley Publishers.

Milner, J. and O'Byrne, P. (2002) *Assessment in Social Work*, 2nd edn, Basingstoke, Palgrave Macmillan.

Thompson, N. (2002) *People Skills*, 2nd edn, Basingstoke, Palgrave Macmillan. Chapter 19.

Varma, V. P. (ed.) (1990) *The Management of Children with Emotional and Behavioural Difficulties*, London, Routledge

Varma, V. P. (ed.) (1992) *The Secret Life of Vulnerable Children*, London, Routledge.

Chapter 4

Communication Skills

Introduction

Communication is a central feature not only of the caring professions, but also of most, if not all, activities and occupations which involve people. As Good (2001) comments:

> Human language and the ways in which we use it lie at the very heart of our social lives. It is through communication with one another that personal relationships, communities and societies are made and maintained, and it is through these social networks and relationships that we become who we are. (p. 76)

The success or failure of much of what we try to achieve in working in group care depends to a large extent on how well we interact with people – how well we communicate. This refers to communicating with the children and young people in our care as well as the adults involved in the partnership network. It is therefore important to be clear about what are the hallmarks of good communication and what are the pitfalls or barriers which can stand in the way of effective communication.

There are skills which can be learned and practised which can help you to communicate more successfully and thereby contribute to improving the quality and standard of your work. The focus in this chapter is therefore on developing a framework which will help you to improve your communication skills.

This framework consists of three main elements:

- verbal skills: talking and listening – with individuals and small groups;
- writing skills: recording information, writing reports and so on; and
- non-verbal skills: making positive use of body language.

We shall consider each of these in turn and look at ways in which these skills can be developed or improved. I shall provide a number of pointers and guidelines for you and encourage you to try these out in your day-to-day work with children and young people.

Each of the three skill areas will have its own set of issues and specific concerns. However, there are also common themes which apply across all three areas. One of these commonalities which is particularly significant is that of sensitivity. Each of the three areas requires a degree of sensitivity if communication is to be effective and successful. It involves being sensitive to the 'signals' given by the people we deal with, and indeed the signals we give to others, whether intentionally or not. Some of the exercises in this chapter are therefore geared towards helping you develop a greater awareness of communication issues and consequently a greater degree of sensitivity.

Sensitivity is particularly important in communicating with children. As Crompton (1990) puts it, it is necessary to 'attend to' children:

> Effective communication can be achieved only when adults really attend to children, which includes recognising such feelings as fear of failure and frustration. Only really looking, listening

and feeling can lead to understanding. Real communication may be very costly to the caring adult in terms of energy, self-knowledge and emotion. But paying the price may help a child to live. (p. 83)

The value and significance of these comments should become clearer as we work our way through each of the three sections which follow.

Verbal skills

Language and speech are very complex matters which have fascinated philosophers, linguists and many others for centuries. Fortunately, we do not need to delve too deeply into these complications and intricacies to be able to make steps forward in our understanding and use of spoken communication.

Ironically, one of the key elements of getting your message across is being able to listen. Listening skills are an essential part of verbal communication for the simple reason that if you do not listen to others, they are far less likely to listen to you. If, however, you are able to show that you are listening, this opens the channels of communication and allows 'engagement' to take place. In order to communicate well with others we need to be able to 'engage' with them, to develop a communicative bond. Showing good listening skills is part and parcel of this. But what does good listening consist of? We can break it down into its component parts as follows:

1. *Acknowledgement* This can be verbal or non-verbal (smiles, nods, eye contact and so on). It is good to begin with acknowledgement, but it also needs to be used intermittently throughout the conversation (to prevent giving the impression that you have lost interest).
2. *Physical setting* This means ensuring that physical barriers to communications are removed. These would include: not competing with a television set or other distraction; ensuring privacy where this is needed; using appropriate seating, and so on (see also the section below on non-verbal communication).
3. *Emotional climate* This involves being sensitive to the emotional dimension of your inter-actions, in relation to both yourself (if you are anxious, angry or even elated, this can easily be interpreted as being preoccupied and therefore not listening) and the person or persons you are conversing with (see the discussion below on acknowledging feelings).
4. *Time* Good listening takes time. If you give the impression that you are in a hurry, you will also give the impression that you are not able or willing to listen. If you do not genuinely

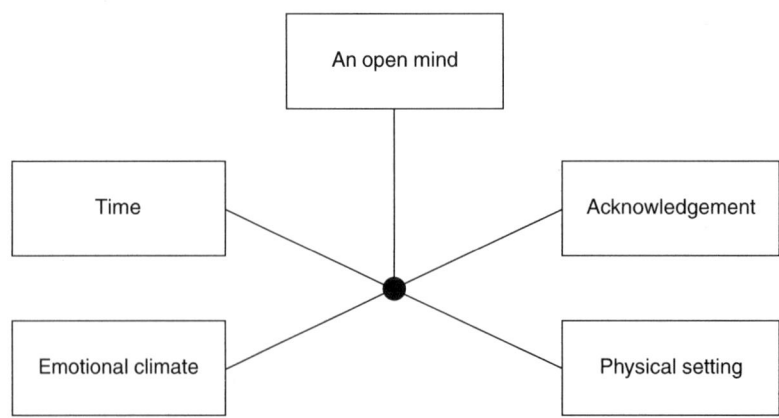

Figure 4.1   The components of effective listening

have time to listen (for example, when you are just about to take another child for a dental appointment), it is wise to be honest and direct about this and perhaps arrange a time when you can talk together properly.

5. *An open mind* One major and significant barrier to effective listening is that of preconceptions. We can easily jump to conclusions on the basis of prejudice and preconceptions rather than actually listen to what is being said to us. In particular, sexist and racist stereotypes can distort our attempts to communicate.

There are many other aspects of effective listening, but these are the five main areas we need to tackle. But, of course, understanding what these components are is not enough to make us effective listeners. We need to be able to relate the theory to practice. Exercise 4.1 has been designed to help you move in that direction.

Exercise 4.1

This is an exercise that can be done as a 'one-off' or it is something you can do over and over again to improve your skills and sensitivity. Choose a situation when two or more people are conversing. It may be a formal discussion (for example, in a meeting) or just a social chat (during a coffee break, for example).

Are the participants listening to each other? How do you know? What signs of listening can you observe? Can you relate these to the five components outlined above?

Use a separate sheet of paper to jot down notes during or after your observations.

Once you have completed this exercise, you should be in a position to start practising your own listening skills.

A further important aspect of verbal communication which complements good listening is that of reflecting feelings. By acknowledging how someone appears to be feeling you can facilitate communication in a number of ways:

- showing concern and compassion (and thereby contributing to the process of 'engagement' discussed above);
- clearing up potential misunderstandings (for example, where you have misinterpreted how someone appears to be feeling);
- helping the person(s) you are speaking to recognise their own feelings and 'move on' – that is, preventing strong feelings from blocking communications.

Reflecting feelings is therefore an important part of verbal communication, especially when the emotional dimension is a key part of the conversation as, for example, when counselling a child or young person:

> Successful reflection of feelings is a delicate and sensitive skill which needs to be nurtured and developed. An example of this skill in practice would be where, in response to a remark made in a tone of anger the counsellor makes a comment along the lines of 'You seem to be quite angry. Do you want to talk about what's bothering you?' This type of response both shows empathy with the client and feeds back important information. For example, the client may not have realised he/she was expressing anger as is often the case when emotions 'creep in' to our communications without our realising it. (Thompson, 1991, pp. 36–7)

The issue of reflecting feelings leads us into other aspects of speech and language. The emotional content of our communications can be conveyed in a number of ways: tone, pitch, speech, register, loudness and so on. In other words, it's not just what you say, it's the way that you say it.

It is worth considering each of these aspects in turn, as they are an important part of how we get our message across (or fail to):

- *Tone* This is a major feature of verbal communication and reveals a great deal about our emotional state. Tone of voice can range from warm, loving and sympathetic, at one extreme, to hostile, aggressive and threatening at the other.
- *Pitch* This is part of 'intonation' and is used, for example, to distinguish between a statement and a question (questions tend to end with rising pitch). Pitch can also give us clues about a person's emotional state. For example, rapid or exaggerated pitch changes can indicate fear or agitation, or a tendency to make only minor pitch changes can indicate depression.
- *Speed* How quickly or slowly we speak also gives clues about our feelings. An inappropriate speed can also act as a barrier to communication – too slow and people are distracted or lose interest; too fast can be irritating or difficult to understand.
- *Register* This refers to the level of formality. The words we use or the style of language we adopt tend to vary according to circumstances and what we see as the appropriate level of formality. There is quite a skill in judging the appropriate 'register' to use according to the 'rules' and expectations of the culture and society we live in. It is interesting to note, for example, that people often tend to be more formal on the telephone than they would be on a face-to-face basis.
- *Loudness* Speaking in a loud voice can indicate anger, assertion of authority and so on. Similarly, speaking quietly or softly can indicate gentleness, concern or a lack of confidence. Sometimes we can begin speaking loudly and assuredly but then trail off as we lose confidence in what we are saying (for example, when we realise that we have made a mistake).

Exercise 4.2

Make a tape recording of one or more conversations between yourself and another person or persons (don't forget to ask their permission before you record them).

Play the recording(s) back and listen carefully, paying close attention to tone, pitch, speed, register and loudness. What can you learn about your own style of verbal communication. Make some notes in the space below. It would be helpful to discuss your findings with a few people who know you well and see what their perceptions are.

Before moving on to consider written communication, it would be helpful to focus explicitly on guidelines for effective verbal communication. These guidelines would include:

1. Make sure you are listening and that the people you are communicating with know that you are listening.
2. Remember to reflect feelings as and when appropriate – for example, when dealing with a distressed or angry child.
3. Pay attention to tone, pitch, speed, register and loudness – your own and other people's.
4. Try to be as clear as possible. Avoid, as far as you can, ambiguity or vagueness. Try to be specific and explicit.
5. Be careful in your use of questions. For example, in trying to encourage a withdrawn child to speak, it is better to use open-ended questions, rather than closed ones (those which require a yes/no answer).
6. Be sensitive to cultural differences when dealing with people from an ethnic group different from your own. Speech customs vary from culture to culture.

7. Similarly, pay attention to different patterns of communication which may arise when speaking with someone whose first language is not English. Beware of the common prejudice that a less than perfect grasp of English is a sign of low intelligence.
8. Beware of using sexist, racist or other discriminatory forms of language. For example, using words like 'chairman' (rather than the more neutral 'chair' or 'chairperson') reinforces the notion that positions of power are reserved for men, thus potentially alienating any women you are attempting to communicate with.
9. Remember, when communicating with children, to gear yourself to their developmental level. Beware of 'talking down' to an older child or talking 'over the head' of a younger child.
10. Take account of hearing impairment. Some degree of hearing loss is not uncommon in many children and adults. Often people make the mistake of shouting when all that may be needed is to speak clearly and perhaps slightly more loudly than usual.

Exercise 4.3

Consider each of the ten guidelines above and think of a concrete example of a situation in which they each applied. Then, having done this, compare notes with a colleague (or someone else whose opinion you value) and see what examples they can think of. If you have time, repeat this exercise with other colleagues or arrange to discuss it in a small group. In this way you will gradually build up a greater sensitivity.

Above all, the main practice guideline is quite simply: be sensitive. Through a raised level of awareness and practice you can become gradually more sensitive to the subtleties of language and learn to use it as effectively as possible.

Writing skills

Much of our communication is in writing, a fact which raises a number of issues. First, writing is more permanent; it can stay 'on file' for years. Second, written communication is more open to misinterpretation, as it does not carry with it many of the 'clues' and reinforcements of verbal and non-verbal communication. This is one reason why we need to be especially careful in communicating in writing – to ensure that we are getting the right message across. Third, written communication tends to be more formal and official. Fourth, due to a combination of the above three points, putting things in writing can cause a great deal of anxiety – for example, when preparing a report for court.

Exercise 4.4

What writing tasks does your job involve? Make a list of the various ways in which you are expected to communicate in writing. Then consider whether there is a particular format you are expected to follow (for example, court reports, review reports, child protection conference reports). If you are unclear about these expectations, take this opportunity to seek clarification from your line manager or a senior colleague.

Because these are important issues, this section attempts to help you develop skills in the sometimes difficult and worrying task of communicating in writing. We begin by looking at the purpose of 'putting it in writing'.

Purpose

When it is necessary to communicate in writing, it is important to be clear about why you are doing so, as this will have an influence on how you do it, what style, length, form and so on your communication takes. A major part of this issue of 'purpose' is the question: 'Who is it you are writing for?' That is, who or what is your target readership? This is very important, as a mistake at this stage could be very problematic and embarrassing – for example, if you were to prepare a report for a case conference in the style and format of a court report. It is therefore important to be clear right at the start about your purpose in writing and, in particular, the style and format you will adopt. Many reports have a set format which you are expected or obliged to follow. Exercise 4.4 should help you clarify what these are.

Perhaps the most important part of format is structure. Different reports will require different structures and so it is difficult to generalise. However, as a rule, it is worth following this simple formula:

- *Introduction* This is where you spell out what the report is about, the target readership and so on. It sets the scene and helps the reader to get a mental picture of what is to come, thus helping to aid understanding.
- *Main body* This contains the main substance of your report, the set of points you are trying to make. As far as possible, these points should be arranged in a logical order so that they provide a structured line of argument rather than an apparently random 'shopping list' of points.
- *Conclusion* The aim here is to draw your report to a logical close. It is therefore important to be clear about the purpose of the report, otherwise you will not know what is an appropriate conclusion. A brief summary is usually helpful.

This framework can be summarised as follows:

Say what you're going to say.	[Introduction]
Say it.	[Main body]
Say what you've said.	[Conclusion]

In order to write a structured report it is necessary to do some planning in advance. It is therefore helpful to make some notes and plan an outline before you start writing. Knowing what you are trying to say makes it an awful lot easier to say it!

The guiding principle in planning a report must be that of purpose: Why am I writing this report? What am I trying to achieve? What this means is that you should consider, in advance, whether your task is to:

- provide factual information only (for example, concerning a child protection incident);
- make a judgement (for example, concerning whether you feel a child is ready to return home);
- offer recommendations (for example, concerning the contents of a written agreement).

Expression

The basic rule here is to ensure that you express yourself clearly. Some people try hard to express themselves in an elegant or impressive way. This is fine if you can do this and write clearly but the very real danger to be wary of is to go for elegance at the expense of clarity. An example of this would be where someone reads a report and then comments: 'This sounds very impressive but what does it mean?' Similarly, beware of flowery language. This can not only reduce clarity, but also comes across as pretentious and irritating.

> ### *Exercise 4.5*
>
> Choose a book, more or less any book will do. Select a page at random and start to read it. But, instead of concentrating on the content of the writing, focus your attention on the punctuation. Each time you come across an item of punctuation, try to work out what it is there for. What purpose is it serving? Carry on doing this until you've covered at least one page of writing and preferably several.
>
> If you don't feel very confident about using punctuation, you would do well to repeat this exercise from time to time and gradually build up your awareness of how punctuation works.

Clear written communication is based on:

- avoiding ambiguous words or phrases;
- being specific and avoiding vagueness (for example,'a lot' could refer to 5, 55, 5,000 or even more);
- not writing in long, cumbersome or convoluted sentences;
- breaking up the report into clear paragraphs;
- the effective use of punctuation;
- and so on.

The effective use of punctuation is something a lot of people find difficult. Some pointers may therefore prove useful.

Commas often prove to be problematic. It should be remembered that a comma indicates a pause. It is often used to separate off different parts of a sentence ('clauses'), and so its presence or absence can affect the meaning of a sentence. For example, consider the difference between: 'He knows I think' and 'He knows, I think'.

Apostrophes can also affect the meaning of a sentence if they are not used correctly. They usually indicate possession. For example, 'the cat's tail' means 'the tail of the cat'. An apostrophe comes before the s with a singular noun, as in the example above, but after the s with a plural: 'the cats' tails'. As with commas, it is important to get this right, as an apostrophe in the wrong place could significantly change the meaning of what you are trying to say. For example, 'She praised her son's efforts' refers to one son, whereas 'She praised her sons' efforts' refers to two or more children. If you ignore the apostrophe altogether: 'She praised her sons efforts', you are being ambiguous and inviting misinterpretation.

As with verbal communication, a key guiding principle is that of developing sensitivity. We usually take punctuation for granted but, if we are to minimise the chances of our writing being misinterpreted, we need to become more sensitive to how punctuation is used. Exercise 4.5 is designed to help you take a step in that direction.

There are parallels between what we have said about punctuation and what we need to say about spelling. Poor spelling not only causes a bad impression but also increases the chances of misinterpretation. For example, there is a big difference in meaning between: to affect [= to have an effect on someone or something] and to effect [= to bring about].

Again, it is a matter of developing a sensitivity to how words are spelled. The basic rule should be: if in doubt, look it up in a dictionary. It is wise to make sure you have a dictionary available.

Relevance

One commonly encountered problem with written communication is the inclusion of irrelevant material and/or the omission of important points or information. This brings us to the thorny question of: How do you know what is relevant and what is not? Unfortunately, there is no simple, foolproof answer to this. Sometimes a point can seem to be of little relevance at the time of writing a particular report but, at the meeting for which the report was prepared, it may take on a new significance. Similarly, points which seemed to be very relevant at the time of writing can be set in a new context or be overtaken by events and thus fade into the background.

However, despite the absence of a foolproof answer, there are two pointers that can help you go some way towards establishing what is relevant and what is not:

- Relevance depends on the purpose of the communication. What is relevant for a review meeting may not be relevant for a child protection conference.
- In considering whether or not to include a particular point or piece of information, ask yourself the questions: How will this be useful if I include it? How would it help? Would it cause any problems if I didn't include it?

If you are in any doubt about the relevance or otherwise of a particular issue, these two pointers should be of help. Don't forget to ask the advice of a colleague or your line manager if you feel you need it.

Practical guidelines

Many people find written work difficult but, with practice and guidance, it does get a lot easier. The following practical guidelines are intended to help your skill development in conjunction with the opportunities to practise you will get as part of your job.

1. Make sure that the format, tone and so on, are appropriate to the purpose.
2. Remember to plan in advance what you are going to say and how you are going to say it.
3. Present your points in a logical order within a structured framework (this is where careful planning pays dividends).
4. Concentrate on expressing yourself clearly. Beware of vagueness and ambiguity or long, convoluted sentences. Reading out loud to yourself what you have written can help you to check that it is clearly written.
5. Avoid discriminatory or offensive language. Beware of reinforcing racist, sexist or disablist stereotypes.
6. Make sure you don't distract or mislead your reader with errors of punctuation, spelling and so on. It is important to create a professional impression.
7. Remember to proofread what you have written. A typing error or omitted word could, in certain cases, prove very problematic and embarrassing. Your well-chosen phrase could be rendered meaningless by an unspotted error.
8. Distinguish between fact and opinion. That is, if you are offering an opinion (rather than stating a known fact) it is important that you make it clear that you are doing so. You will need to use phrases like: 'I believe (this to be the case)' or 'I feel this is the case'.
9. Arrange to have a dictionary or even a thesaurus on hand. Don't risk misleading your reader by using the wrong word when a moment spent consulting a dictionary could remove this risk.
10. Try to get to grips with the thorny question of relevance. Think carefully about what should, and should not, be included.

Exercise 4.6

Ask your line manager or another senior colleague to let you have a look at what he or she regards as examples of good written communications (for example, review reports). Have a close look at them and see if you can work out what is good about them. Make some notes below. Once you've done this, compare notes with the person who provided the reports for you and see what tips you can learn from this.

Non-verbal communication

In addition to what we say and write we also communicate in a variety of 'non-verbal' ways. This is often known as 'body language' and is often discussed in a lighthearted way, as if it were just an interesting side issue rather than a very important aspect of interpersonal communication. We need to be wary of this and recognise that the various forms of non-verbal communication can play a central role in our dealings with children and adults. We therefore explore here how an understanding of non-verbal communication (or NVC, for short) can be used to improve the effectiveness of our communication.

Once again there will be a focus on developing sensitivity for, as I have argued previously, 'although we all learn the basics of non-verbal communication as part of the process of growing up, there is much to be gained by learning to use these skills at a more advanced level' (Thompson, 2003b, p. 132).

Non-verbal communication is quite subtle and complex and we are very rarely directly aware of the impact it has on us. It is therefore important to understand how it works and how it can get in the way of our attempts to get our message across. Non-verbal behaviour consists of a variety of elements (see Figure 4.2) and we shall look at each of these in turn.

1. Facial expression

The most obvious examples of this are smiles and frowns. However, we should note that there is much more to it than this. Our faces can show a whole range of emotions: pleasure, displeasure, anger, sadness, excitement, puzzlement, concern, humour and so on.

Sometimes our facial expression will contradict what we are saying. For example, our words may say: 'I am happy that ...', whereas the look on our face may show that we are far from happy. The important point to note here is that, where a verbal and non-verbal communication are in conflict, it is the non-verbal communication which tends to dominate. That is, NVC is more powerful than verbal communications and will 'overrule' them to a large extent. It is for this reason that it is important that we become sensitive to our own facial expressions and what message we are giving to people, as well as being able to understand the subtleties of other people's facial expressions.

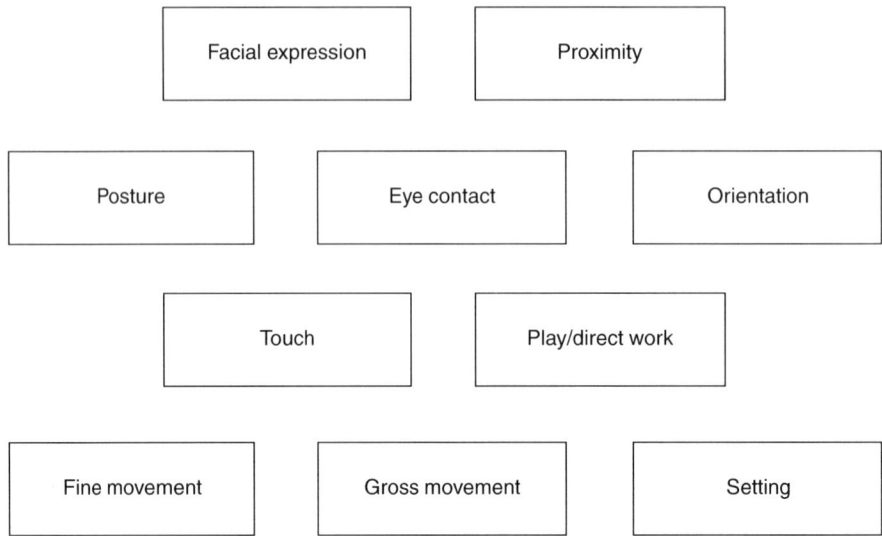

Figure 4.2: Types of non-verbal communication

2. *Proximity*

This refers to how close or far apart we stand or sit in relation to one another. For example, too far apart can seem unfriendly, too close can seem threatening and overbearing. What is considered appropriate can vary from situation to situation and is also dependent on gender and culture. There is no simple or clear-cut rule for judging what is an appropriate distance. Once again it is a matter of sensitivity – becoming more aware of the significance of proximity. Exercise 4.7 is intended to help you develop such an awareness.

Exercise 4.7

For this exercise you will need to observe other people's body language. Choose a number of situations in which two or more people are conversing. Take note of how close they are together. Does the proximity change according to the situation? For example, do more formal occasions mean that people do not get as close? Are there any gender differences? Can you notice any occasions when someone seemed uncomfortable about the proximity? Make some notes on a separate sheet of paper. This is a simple exercise which does not take up much time, so you would do well to try it over and over again and gradually build up skills in 'reading' body language.

---

3. *Posture*

This relates to our 'body attitude'. It is shown by whether we sit back or lean forward, whether we cross our legs and so on. Posture is usually a good indicator of two things – how relaxed the person is and what his or her attitude towards you is (hostile/friendly, formal/informal, attentive/inattentive and so on). Being able to recognise the 'signals' given by posture can be very helpful in giving you indications about the other person's attitude or feelings towards you. It can be a good early detector of potential violence or aggression. Similarly, you can use your own posture to 'set the scene' to establish the tone of your inter-action. For example, if you adopt a relaxed posture, this can help the other person to relax.

4. *Eye contact*

The amount and nature of eye contact between people is very socially significant. Little or no eye contact is usually a sign of timidity or a reluctance to become engaged in conversation. Prolonged or intense eye contact usually indicates threat or aggression. Given these two extremes, it is important to be able to get the right balance. The right amount of eye contact communicates warmth, interest and concern: too little suggests a lack of interest and too much can be intrusive and overbearing. Once again there is no simple or clear-cut formula to follow in determining what is the appropriate level of eye contact, although observation and practice will pay dividends.

5. *Orientation*

This refers to what direction you face in relation to the person you speak to. For example, turning away from someone tends to suggest rejection or lack of interest. Speaking over your shoulder can have a similar effect:

> Imagine a nursery worker sorting through some equipment on a shelf. A small boy comes up and pulls at his trouser leg. The worker speaks to the child over his shoulder without turning to face him. This gives the message that the worker is not willing, at that moment, to give full attention to the child. (Petrie, 1989, p. 10)

Our 'orientation' can therefore give powerful messages even though we may not be aware of them or intend them. Once again, being able to 'read' these signs is an important part of effective communication.

6. *Touch*

Touch is probably the most powerful NVC. If used carefully, touch can be very useful and effective. However, it can also be problematic if used unthinkingly:

> Touch can be particularly effective but a note of caution is called for. Touch is a form of communication and so can easily be misinterpreted. We therefore need to be very clear about the message touch is conveying and that this is supported or confirmed verbally. Touch can be either very supportive or an oppressive invasion of personal space. If construed as the latter a lot of harm can be done. Where the issue arises between a male worker and a female client, the question of sexual harassment can arise. This is a very real issue and a great cause for concern; it should not be dismissed or trivialised. I would therefore counsel caution by advising that touch be used selectively and sensitively. (Thompson, 1991, p. 37)

These points are very relevant to dealing with children who have been abused, particularly those who have been sexually abused.

7. *Play/direct work*

There is a long tradition in social care of communicating with children through play. This is often known as 'direct work' and includes drawing and painting and so on, as well as games and toys. This form of communication can be planned and deliberate as, for example, when anatomically correct dolls are used as part of a child protection investigation.

Alternatively, important communication can arise spontaneously through play. For example, children can use play to get a message across which is perhaps too painful to put into words. This is often the case with child abuse disclosures, as we shall see in Chapter 5. Direct work is a skilled area of child care practice, with its own literature and specialised training.

8. *Fine movements*

This refers to gestures and other such 'fine' movements of parts of the body. Many of these are deliberate (for example, beckoning) whereas others tend to occur more spontaneously, perhaps even unintentionally:

> sometimes people do not realise that their movements give messages. For example, a mother may smile when you say you are sorry for keeping her waiting and say 'It's quite all right, I'm not in a hurry', but give away her true feelings by tapping her foot. (Petrie, 1989, p. 10)

This is another example of how, where verbal and non-verbal communications contradict each other, the NVC is the more powerful and influential.

9. *Gross movements*

This refers to larger-scale body movements which, more often than not, tend to be quite dramatic in their impact. This would include: walking away/leaving the room, pushing, hitting, grabbing and so on. Acts of aggression and violence are, after all, examples of very strong and extreme non-verbal communications. For example, a child who lashes out may be expressing an emotion (for example, frustration) which he or she feels unable to express in any other way. We shall return to this point in Chapter 8.

10. *Setting*

The place and circumstances in which we choose to communicate can be very significant and a powerful form of communication in their own right. For example, if we discuss a sensitive or delicate matter with a child in the presence of other people, we may, albeit inadvertently, be giving the message that the issues are not important, that they do not merit a one-to-one discussion in private. Similarly, what you perceive as just a 'chat' with a young person in the office may actually be perceived by the young person as something much more formal and official – precisely because it takes place in the office. We therefore need to be careful about the setting in which communication takes place, as this can be a powerful influence on how our communications are received.

In interpreting non-verbal communication we need to bear in mind the principle that we are looking for patterns of communication rather than individual 'tell-tale' signs. As Honey (1988) comments:

> The risk of a wrong interpretation can be reduced by resisting the considerable temptation to jump to a conclusion based on the observation of isolated pieces of behaviour. It is much safer (but nothing will guarantee you get it right) to base an interpretation on a number of different non-verbal behaviours that fit together into a coherent pattern or cluster. (pp. 156–7)

In effect, this is what Exercise 4.8 is geared towards – becoming sensitive to patterns of non-verbal communication so that our understanding of these can be put to maximum positive effect in our dealings with children, and young people and other adults in the child care system.

Exercise 4.8

This exercise follows on from Exercise 4.7. Your task is once again to observe people interacting and take note of the examples of non-verbal communications that you witness. This time, however, you should try to take account of all ten of the areas outlined above (and any others you may become aware of). You may find it helpful to make some notes.

Conclusion

Communication is a fundamental aspect of caring work and so we ignore these important issues at our peril. It is also a vast, complex and intricate area of study so there is always something new to learn, always an extra dimension to explore. Fortunately, this is also the strong point of developing communication skills – it is a fascinating and absorbing process and many people become very keen and excited about furthering their knowledge, understanding and skills. In particular, you should perhaps be warned that observing non-verbal communication can be addictive! You can find yourself getting hooked on making sense of the subtleties of body language.

This chapter cannot, in itself, make you a more effective communicator, but it has, we hope, given you some of the tools for developing the knowledge, skills and sensitivity you need to get the best out of your interactions with others. Many of the issues to do with communication are particularly relevant to child abuse. Communication involves a significant element of faith and trust, but child abuse situations are usually characterised by a breakdown or betrayal of trust. This raises important questions for child care workers, and so it is to some of these that we turn in Chapter 5.

Guide to further learning

Communication: general

Burnard, P. (1992) *Communicate!*, London, Edward Arnold.

Crompton, M. (1990) *Attending to Children*, London, Edward Arnold.

Hargie, O., Saunders, S. and Dickson, D. (eds) (1994) *Social Skills in Interpersonal Communication*, 3rd edn, London, Routledge.

Thompson, N. (2003) *Communication and Language: A Handbook of Theory and Practice*, Basingstoke, Palgrave Macmillan.

Verbal skills

Fontana, D. (1990) *Social Skills at Work*, London, Routledge, especially Part 4.

Thompson, N. (2002) *People Skills*, 2nd edn, Basingstoke, Palgrave Macmillan. Chapters 10 and 13.

Thompson, N. (2003) *Communication and Language: A Handbook of Theory and Practice*, Basingstoke, Palgrave Macmillan, Chapters 4 and 6.

Writing skills

There are a wide range of popular books on grammar, punctuation, spelling and so on, available in bookshops. See also:

O'Rourke, L. (2002) *For the Record: Recording Skills Training Manual*, Lyme Regis, Russell House Publishing.

Thompson, N. (2002) *People Skills*, 2nd edn, Basingstoke, Palgrave Macmillan. Chapter 12.

Thompson, N. (2003) *Communication and Language: A Handbook of Theory and Practice*, Basingstoke, Palgrave Macmillan, Chapters 3 and 7.

Non-verbal communication

Chazan, S.E. (2002) *Profiles of Play: Assessing and Observing Structure and Process in Play Therapy*, London, Jessica Kingsley Publishers.

Thompson, N. (2002) *People Skills*, 2nd edn, Basingstoke, Palgrave Macmillan, Chapter 11.

Thompson, N. (2003) *Communication and Language: A Handbook of Theory and Practice*, Basingstoke, Palgrave Macmillan, Chapters 4 and 6.

West, J. (1992) *Child-Centred Play Therapy*, London, Edward Arnold.

Chapter 5

Dealing with Abuse

Introduction

It is understandable that child abuse should be such a cause of concern for group care staff as, indeed, it is for other professionals who work with children. It is a very emotive area and one which gives rise to considerable anxiety. No amount of training, experience or skill will take away the demands of child protection work, but this chapter can at least go some way towards equipping you to deal with these demands as effectively and painlessly as possible.

We shall cover three aspects of dealing with child abuse. First, we shall consider the difficult task of recognising or detecting abuse. I shall outline the main potential 'indicators' of abuse and consider the best way of coping with the complexities involved in using them. Second, we shall look at what needs to be done when abuse is suspected or confirmed – the procedures that need to be followed. Third, we shall examine ways of working with children who have been abused, particularly those whose behaviour, relationships and emotional responses have been seriously affected by the trauma of the abuse.

But, before tackling these issues, there is a further matter we need to be clear about. We need to establish what we mean by the term 'child abuse':

> The question of what constitutes child abuse is a major one which has attracted considerable attention. What makes the issues so complex is that child abuse is socially constructed; that is, what is seen as abuse is defined by social mores and cultural values rather than in any absolute sense – it can be seen to vary from culture to culture and historically within the same culture. (Thompson, 1992b, p. 14)

What this suggests is that there can be no simple, clear-cut definition of child abuse which applies to all societies at all times, the Children Act 1989 uses the key concept of 'significant harm'. Children are deemed to be in need of protection when they are suffering, or are likely to suffer, significant harm. This is still quite vague and lacking in precision (when does harm become significant harm?) but it does, at least, give us a framework to work with.

Child abuse was for many years divided up into four categories:

Physical abuse: Injury or physical harm which is not of an accidental nature. As we shall see below, certain types of injury are more likely to give rise to suspicion than others.

Sexual abuse: The Department of Health (1999) defines sexual abuse as:

> forcing or enticing a child or young person to take part in sexual activities, whether or not the child is aware of what is happening. The activities may involve physical contact, including penetrative (e.g. rape or buggery) or non-penetrative acts. They may include non-contact activities, such as involving children in looking at, or in the production of, pornographic material or watching sexual activities or encouraging children to behave in sexually inappropriate ways. (p. 6)

Emotional abuse: Persistent or severe treatment of a child (for example, rejection or constant criticism) which is likely to have an adverse effect on emotional development.

Neglect: Significant harm caused, or likely to be caused, to a child by parental failure to meet basic needs (food, warmth, protection and so on). In young children, this often results in a 'failure to thrive' (that is, developmental milestones are not attained – see Chapter 2).

In addition to these long-standing forms of abuse, in recent years we have become acutely aware of another significant form of abuse:

Institutional abuse: Harm to children and young people who are inadequately cared for and/or directly abused in children's homes, residential schools and so on.

We should also note that there are two less well-publicised forms of child abuse. The first of these is known as 'system abuse'. This refers to the type of situation in which the involvement of officialdom can prove as abusive – or even more so – as the initial abuse, or can create an abusive situation where none existed before (as, for example, when a false allegation causes considerable distress for the child and family). This concept raises the question: How do we prevent child protection interventions from causing children undue stress and suffering?

This, in turn, raises a major dilemma and underlines clearly and emphatically the complexities of dealing with child abuse. There is no simple or straightforward solution to this problem, but what is clear is that we must be very sensitive in how we respond to allegations, how we handle situations when abuse is confirmed, and how we deal with the aftermath for the child or children concerned. The child protection system can, in itself, be abusive and oppressive, and so it is important that we think before we act and that we become wary of the pitfalls.

The seventh and final form of abuse is what we could call 'social' abuse. Writers such as Loney (1989) point out that we react very strongly to situations where children receive minor injuries and yet, as a society, we allow so many children to be abused by virtue of experiencing poverty, deprivation, homelessness, inadequate health care and so on. This reflects our tendency to see child abuse as a matter of individual 'pathology' and to fail to take account of wider social, political and economic factors.

What this approach teaches us is that a focus on individual factors without reference to wider social patterns and issues represents a narrow and blinkered approach. We need to think not only of individual cases, but also of the recurring patterns and themes which can give us a wider and better informed picture of this complex and difficult aspect of child care practice.

These, then, are the seven main forms of abuse, although, as we have commented, the latter two tend to receive far less attention than the first five. The picture is already starting to get complicated and involved, and so it will perhaps be helpful for you to clarify your own thoughts on the subject before going any further. Exercise 5. 1 is designed to help you with this.

Exercise 5.1

Spend a little time thinking about your own view of child abuse. What does the term actually mean to you? Jot below some of the key ideas or issues that come to mind. After you've done this, try to think about your own feelings on the matter. What feelings does child abuse evoke in you? Jot them down on a separate piece of paper. (These can be kept confidential if you wish. There is no need for you to share them with others unless you so choose. It is important, however, that you are aware of your own feelings on the matter, as these can have an effect on how you do your job.)

Recognising abuse

First of all, we need to be clear that child abuse is not a 'disease', and so recognising abuse is not simply a matter of looking for particular 'symptoms' (although some of the traditional textbooks do give this misleading impression). There are, however, a number of 'indicators' which can give us clues or point us in the right direction. This section explores what these main indicators are and considers how they can best be used.

Physical signs

Perhaps the most visible indication of abuse is a physical injury, especially where a doctor confirms that the explanation given for the injury is not consistent with the nature or severity of that injury. But note that it is the inconsistency which is a strong indicator of abuse and not the injury itself.

Some types of injury are particularly suspicious – for example, finger bruising or cigarette burns. There is no need for you to be an expert in recognising suspicious marks or injuries, although you would be wise to follow some of the references in the 'Guide to further learning' section in order to familiarise yourself with some of the common worrying physical signs. However, as we shall emphasise below, the underlying principle and practice guideline must be: *if you have any doubts or suspicions, discuss them with a colleague or your line manager*. It is dangerous to ignore potentially worrying warning signs. You will not get into trouble if you raise concerns in good faith, but it is possible that staff who do not raise concerns when they should have done so may face disciplinary proceedings.

Vulnerability factors

Wright *et al.* (1991) list nine sets of factors which may make an abusive situation more likely. These are reproduced in Figure 5.1. We should note, however, that vulnerability factors are not 'symptoms'. They are factors which should alert us to the possibility of abuse, rather than signs that abuse has taken place. We shall return to this point below.

a) A previous incident of child abuse to the child or a sibling;

b) Social stress – unemployment, financial difficulties, inadequate housing and homelessness, the effect of living in high-rise flats, single parenthood;

c) Marital stress – young immature parents, isolation from the extended family;

d) Psychopathic, alcoholic, violent or over-emotional persons;

e) Low intelligence;

f) Unwanted pregnancy and/or rejected child in the family;

g) Any situation which interferes with bonding in the first weeks after birth, such as prematurity or illness;

h) Age of mother – particularly very young mothers;

i) Poor health of mother.

Figure 5.1   Vulnerability factors (Wright *et al.*, 1991)

Behaviour

Often our suspicions of abuse are raised by particular aspects of a child's or young person's behaviour. This can be as a result of an apparently inexplicable change in behaviour – a sudden alteration in characteristic patterns. Or, alternatively it may be as a result of particular behaviours which are, in themselves, potential indicators of an abusive situation. There are many aspects of a child's behaviour that can give rise to suspicions of abuse. However, we shall limit ourselves to just five of these here.

1. Compliance

Often children who have been subjected to abuse will become very compliant. They become eager to please and will sometimes go to extreme lengths to avoid conflict. Such children become very anxious to avoid situations arising where further abuse is likely to arise. They will therefore make great efforts to avoid the need for punishment.

2. Frozen watchfulness

This term describes situations in which children become very wary of adults – they watch anxiously and attentively as if in great fear or trepidation. Such children tend to be quite still and wary, showing themselves to be fearful, suspicious and defensive. For some children, this attitude is visible in response to all adults, whereas for others it applies only to a particular adult or adults – for example, parents.

3. Attention seeking

It is not uncommon for children who have experienced family breakdown to display attention-seeking behaviour, and so this should not always be seen as a sign of abuse. Similarly, children with learning disabilities may engage in a great deal of attention-seeking behaviour. However, the constant need for attention and reassurance can also be an indicator of abuse, a sign of the underlying insecurity that abusive situations can bring about.

4. Disruptive behaviour

Although disruptive behaviour can arise for a variety of reasons, aggression, destructiveness and non-compliance can also be indicative of a situation in which a child or young person has been abused. It is known that abuse can create strong feelings of anger and resentment, and so poor behaviour can be seen as a reflection of such negative feelings.

5. Sexualised behaviour

Children who have been sexually abused will often display inappropriate sexual behaviour. Bannister (1989) gives some examples of this:

> The eight-year old girl who acts as though she were 18 in a sexually provocative way, the four-year old child who grabs the genitals of adults, the 14 year-old boy who seems to have missed out on childhood and is disturbingly 'knowing' may behave in these ways as a result of abuse. (p. 167)

An important point to note here is in relation to people with learning disabilities. It is often the case that children with learning disabilities display sexualised behaviour, even though they may not have been abused.

These, then, are the main behavioural indications of abuse. As with other indicators, though, we should remember that these are not definite 'symptoms'. As I shall emphasise below, indicators are only the beginning of our assessment and not the whole story.

Disclosure

Perhaps the most clear-cut indicator of abuse is a disclosure by the child or young person concerned. He or she may confide in a worker or other person that abuse has occurred. This raises delicate issues of confidentiality, a point to which we shall return below. Whether or not the disclosure is given in confidence, we are duty-bound to respond to it and act in accordance with the Child Protection Procedures, as we shall see in the next section.

Children may make a direct and explicit disclosure. They will, if the circumstances are right, openly talk about the abuse. However, it is sometimes more complex than this and the disclosure is more implicit and indirect. For example, a child may drop hints or skirt round the issue without addressing it directly. This may reflect the child's ambivalence about whether or not it is safe to disclose. Alternatively, it may be part of the child's 'strategy' for finding the right person, the right time and the right circumstances in which to make a disclosure of abuse.

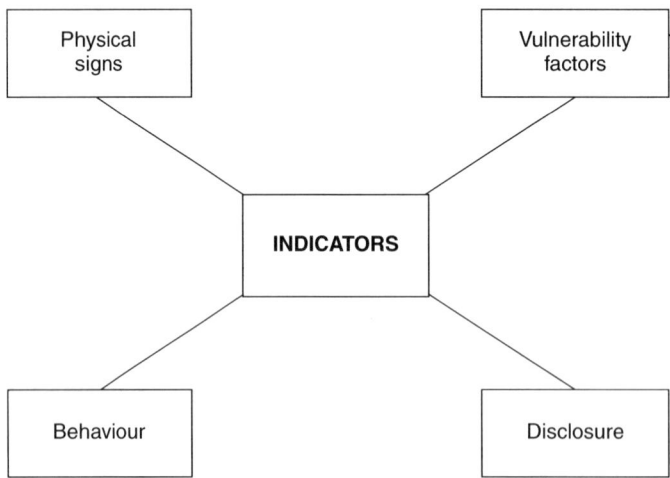

Figure 5.2   Indicators of abuse

Pieces of the jigsaw

Although indicators are very important in recognising, and dealing with, child abuse, we must be careful not to attach too much significance to them. Most of the indicators discussed here can arise for reasons other than abuse; there are few, if any, clear-cut definitive signs of abuse. Unfortunately, there are many cases on record where social work staff, and indeed others within the child protection system, have over-reacted to indications. That is, they have put 2 and 2 together, and made 5.

What we must look for is a pattern of indicators, pieces of a jigsaw that fit together and produce a worrying picture. The difficult task that faces us is to achieve a balance between over-reacting on the one hand, and ignoring vital clues on the other. Because this is such a tricky and demanding task, it is important that we do not shoulder this responsibility alone. An essential part of effective child protection work is that we share our concerns, initially with our colleagues and/or line manager and perhaps later with other professionals within the child protection system (for example, a doctor, a teacher or the police).

Once we start to put the pieces together and our concerns or suspicions start to emerge, it is extremely important that we handle the situation as effectively and sensitively as possible. It is for this reason that official guidelines have been established – to guide staff through the complex and intricate process of dealing with suspicions, allegations and disclosures. It is to this area that we shall be turning shortly, but first, you should spend a little time tackling Exercise 5.2.

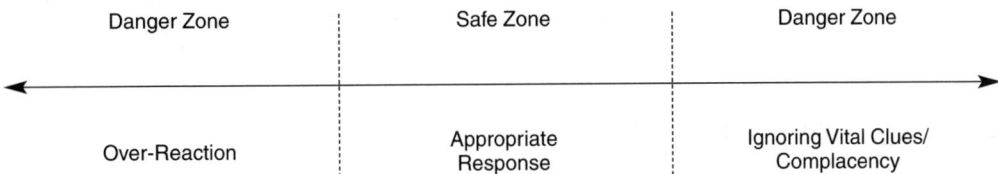

Danger Zone	Safe Zone	Danger Zone
Over-Reaction	Appropriate Response	Ignoring Vital Clues/ Complacency

Figure 5.3   Getting the balance right

Exercise 5.2

Think back over child protection situations you have dealt with in the past (if you have experienced such work) and consider the following questions:

- What indicators were present and how did these come to light?
- How did you (and your colleagues) piece together the jigsaw?
- What was the most difficult part of the process?
- What would you do differently in future?

If you do not have any experience of dealing with such situations, find one or more colleagues who have done so and discuss the four questions above with them.

Child protection procedures

The child protection system is managed by local Area Child Protection Committees (ACPCs) which consist of senior representatives of the key agencies involved (social services, health, education, police and so on). These committees are responsible for overall policies and the procedures which govern how child protection cases must be dealt with.

These procedures are very important indeed. They do not simply provide advice that can be ignored – rather, they provide a pathway that all staff concerned are duty bound to follow. Consequently, it is vitally important that you know what the local procedures are and what duties and responsibilities these place upon you.

Exercise 5.3

This is a simple but essential exercise. It involves:

i)   Ensuring that you have access to a copy of the procedures. There should be at least one copy available in your workplace. Make sure you know where it is.

ii) Reading through the procedures, paying particular attention to those aspects that relate to you and your work. Make sure you are clear what your responsibilities are.

If you have any difficulties with this exercise, make sure you get advice and support from your colleagues or your line manager. Don't take unnecessary risks by carrying on working without being clear about what is expected of you.

A major focus of the child protection procedures is on the need to work together – the need to share views and information, to fit together the pieces of the jigsaw. Dealing with child abuse is potentially very stressful, and so it is essential that we do not tackle this type of work without the support and co-operation of others. It is therefore important to involve other people sooner rather than later. The golden rule must be: *if you have any doubts, suspicions or concerns, consult your line manager at the earliest opportunity*. This is particularly important where a child begins to disclose abuse, whether directly or indirectly. Responding to a child's disclosure is a very responsible and pressurised job, one that we need to consider in more detail.

Dealing with disclosure

The first point we need to be clear about is the limitations of confidentiality. If we have reason to suspect that child abuse is taking place or has taken place, we are duty bound (by the child protection procedures) to report the matter. Where there is a conflict between a child's safety and confidentiality, the child's safety must, of course, come first. As we saw in Chapter 1, the child's welfare is paramount. We therefore need to be wary about agreeing to 'keep secrets' or promise to maintain confidences that we may not be able to keep. It is *essential* that we pass on information relating to a child's safety. If we do not, we may be playing a part (albeit unintentionally perhaps) in contributing to a child being in an unsafe situation.

Such situations need to be handled sensitively with due regard for the child's feelings – and for your own. Disclosure is an emotionally demanding matter for all concerned. Sensitivity also involves winning the trust of the child or young person – and such trust cannot and must not be based on false promises of confidentiality. What needs to be offered in place of such false promises is a genuine promise that you will respect what the child tells you and will do everything you can to support them through dealing with the disclosure and the consequences that may follow on from this (an investigation, a possible case conference, or even a court case).

An important step towards this is to listen carefully to the child. As Furniss (1991) comments:

> When a child makes an intentional full disclosure we need to sit down with the child and talk to her on her own and listen patiently to what the child has to disclose. At the moment of crisis the child will be very open and will be prepared to tell more than at any other time. The first professional who sits down with the child must not panic and must not think how he [*sic*] can instantly involve other professionals at that stage. He should take all the time necessary to listen fully to the child. It is important to realise that the person to whom the child discloses has become the Trusted Person … If the Trusted Person remains with the child throughout the disclosure process none of the facts the child has disclosed will get lost. (p. 215)

Exercise 5.4

If you have dealt with a disclosure before, think back over the experience and consider:

- What do think you did well?
- What did you learn from the experience that will help you handle such situations better in the future?

If you have not had to deal with a disclosure situation, arrange to speak to one or more experienced colleagues who can give you their answers to the questions above.

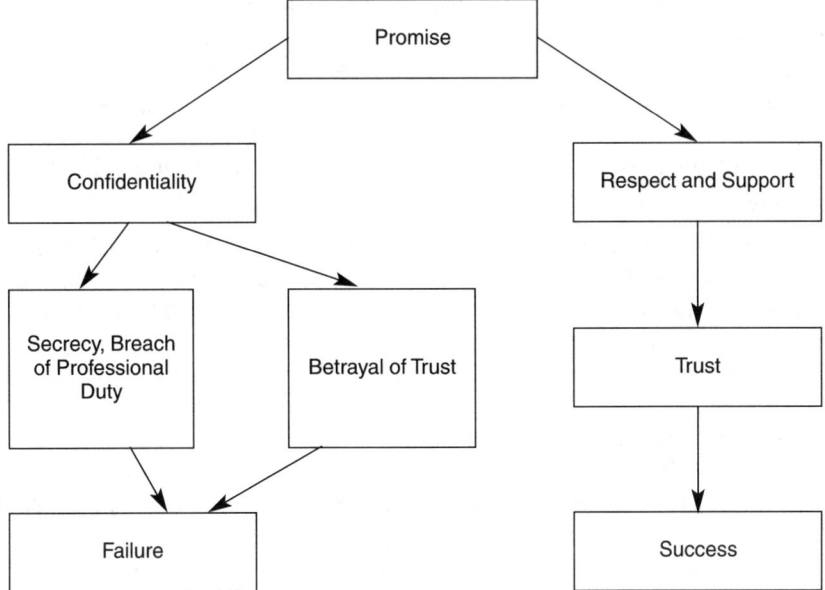

Figure 5.4: The limits of confidentiality

This is quite a demanding task, although staff who become involved in this work often find that they handled the situation better than they had expected – the sense of the situation's importance and seriousness guided them through.

Suspicions about colleagues

It is sadly the case that experience over the years has taught us that we cannot always rely on colleagues to safeguard the welfare of the children and young people in their care. There are now many cases on record of staff who were assumed to be caring, professional staff who have subsequently turned out to be abusers who have exploited their positions of trust. We therefore have to be very careful not to allow complacency to creep in. It is understandable that staff may find it difficult to accept that one or more of their colleagues is a threat to children, but bitter experience has taught us that we cannot afford to ignore any suspicions or warning signs – even if it is our own colleagues who are the basis of our concern.

Whenever we have any concerns or suspicions, we must raise them, even if this relates to a colleague. You should not, however, approach your colleague directly. You should report your concerns to a senior member of staff without alerting the colleague concerned. See your local child protection procedures for further information and guidance.

Dealing with the aftermath

For many children in group care, abuse is a major part of why they are no longer with their families; it is part of a painful history of family breakdown and the loss of important people, relationships and other valued aspects of their lives. It is therefore important that we should not underestimate the traumatic effects that abuse can have on a child or youngster. These include:

- *emotional disturbance* Abuse can generate intense emotions, leaving the child or young person feeling confused, anxious and uncertain. Consequently their emotional response may become extreme, unpredictable or highly variable;

- *anger and/or guilt* The strong feelings generated can be directed outwards as anger, hostility and rejection or directed inwards as guilt, shame and self doubt;
- *depression and low self-esteem* Abuse can leave children feeling degraded, devalued and worthless; when this happens the danger of depression is never far away;
- *lack of trust* Abuse of a child is, of course, also an abuse of trust: it is therefore not surprising that abused children may find it difficult to trust again.

These are some of the major effects but by no means the only ones. There would be little point in attempting to provide a comprehensive list of effects, partly because such a list would be potentially endless and partly because sensitivity to the possible effects is far more important than knowledge of a list.

Indeed, sensitivity is a key aspect of dealing with children who have been abused. However, we must recognise that this is more easily said than done. The development of such sensitivity depends on both experience and training – and the learning and professional development that follow on from these. Responding effectively to the needs of children who have been abused is a demanding task which you cannot be expected to do well right from the start. You will need to build up your skills gradually.

It is also important to remember that your work should be part of a wider multidisciplinary network and so you should not shoulder this responsibility without the support and collaboration of others. It can be dangerous to try and deal with these matters in an isolated way. Working alongside more experienced staff is also a source of useful opportunities for learning and skill development.

Staff dealing with children who have been abused have often been known to express concern about being 'kept in the dark' about plans for how the child is to be helped. For example, where a child or young person receives specialist therapy, the content of that therapeutic programme may be confidential to the therapist in order to allow a relationship based on trust and confidence to develop. However, the fact that such matters are confidential does not mean that you should not be given a clear picture of how you can help or what part you should play in the process. It is therefore important that you are kept informed. If you find you are being kept in the dark, don't be afraid to ask for information or clarification.

As we saw in Chapter 3, effective child care is based on partnership and this must entail those within the partnership being clear about what is happening and what part each person is to play in taking the plan forward. You therefore need to make sure you are aware of what plans and therapeutic programmes exist in relation to each of the children or young people you are working with.

Once again, this is more easily said than done, especially if one or more people within the partnership are not sharing information or are acting in a unilateral way without reference to the others involved in working with the child. However, your ability to work well with the children and young people in your care is likely to be severely impaired if you do not know what is happening. It is therefore important that you seek out the information you need as and when you need it. This is likely to involve you in being assertive, a topic we shall explore in Chapter 8, as it is a key self-management skill.

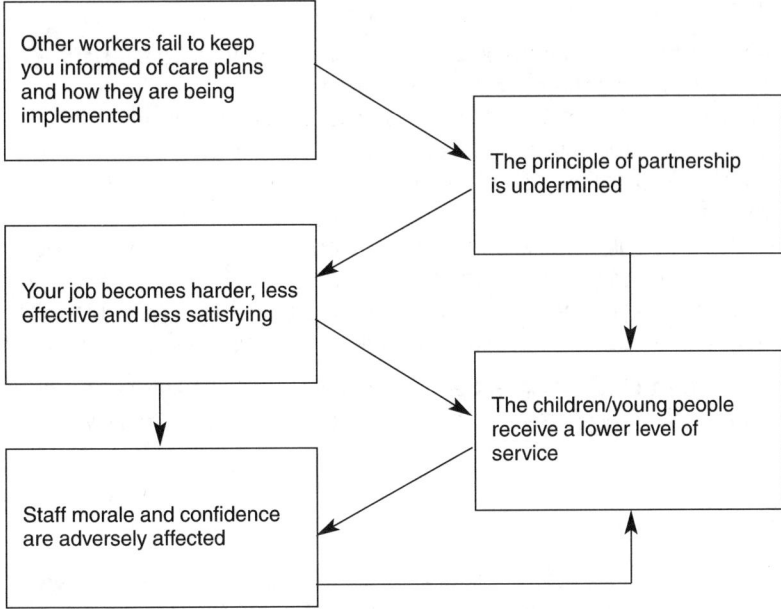

Figure 5.5 Paying the price for being kept in the dark

Dealing with the aftermath of abuse is a multidisciplinary matter and not the responsibility of a single individual. In deciding how best to work with an abused child it is therefore important to ensure that what you are doing is consistent with the care plan agreed and does not undermine the work being undertaken by others. Good communication between professionals is therefore an essential part of helping children cope with the traumatic effects of abuse.

Exercise 5.5

Do you know what the care plans are for the children you work with? If not, do you know how you would go about finding out? These are important questions and ones you should be able to answer in the affirmative. Your task in this exercise is twofold:

1. Make sure you find out what care plans apply to the children you work with and what part you are expected to play, particularly in relation to children who have been abused.
2. Discuss some of these plans with colleagues or your line manager to check that you share the same understanding of what the plans are or that differences of opinion or perspective are identified.

There are no 'right answers' to this exercise, but it will give you the opportunity to develop a better understanding of the importance of care planning.

One consequence of this is that it is vitally important for you to see yourself as part of a wider network of helpers, partly so that you do not undermine the partnership necessary for effective child care and partly so that you do not feel isolated and unsupported in what is, after all, a very demanding and potentially stressful task.

To summarise so far:

- Children who have been abused will often show emotional disturbance, anger, guilt, depression, low self-esteem and a lack of trust.
- Children who have been abused need to be dealt with sensitively.
- Dealing with the aftermath of abuse is a skilled job which requires training and experience; you should not expect to be able to run before you can walk. Be realistic about what you can do.
- Your work is part of a multidisciplinary network and so you need to be clear about where your contribution fits into the overall care plan.
- If you are being kept in the dark about the care plans for a particular child or young person, you will need to be assertive in making sure that this situation is rectified.

Perhaps the two most challenging aspects of this are: dealing with 'acting-out' behaviour and dealing with feelings – our own and those of the children we work with. Let's look at each of these in turn.

'Acting-out'

Abuse can have a profound effect on children, often resulting in some very challenging behaviour which tests or exceeds the boundaries of acceptability. That is, there may be some degree of 'acting-out', as if releasing some of the pressure arising from their previous traumatic experiences. In trying to deal with this type of behaviour, there are a number of points that are worth bearing in mind:

- Children respond positively to having the boundaries of acceptable behaviour clearly spelled out; although we may wish to make some allowances for children who have been abused, we should not go so far as to allow these boundaries to be abandoned. As Barbara Thompson (1990) puts it:

  parents, or others in authority who do not set standards and provide clear limits as to what is acceptable behaviour tend to be seen by children as not caring. The child is therefore unlikely to feel loved if she is given a completely free rein. What is demanded of a carer is that, having set limits, she can monitor them, criticise on occasions when they are overstepped and yet still show love and regard for the youngster who is at one and at the same time determined to prove worthless and desperately wanting to turn out to be good after all. (p. 88)

- Challenging behaviour is often linked to feelings of low self-esteem and worthlessness. It is therefore important to respond to such behaviour in ways that do not reinforce these negative feelings and images. This has two sets of implications:

  1. It is important to focus on, and reinforce, positive aspects of behaviour where possible.
  2. In objecting to negative aspects of behaviour, it is important to make it clear that it is the behaviour that you disapprove of and not the child; children with low self-esteem tend to be sensitive to rejection and will often misinterpret a 'telling-off' as a sign of rejection (see Chapter 7 for a discussion of 'behaviour management').

- As with all behavioural difficulties, it is better, if possible, to prevent confrontation situations arising, rather than try to deal with them when they do arise. A major part of this is being able to respond to the emotional needs of abused children, a point to which we shall return below.

These are some of the significant issues that arise in relation to dealing with 'acting-out' behaviour linked to previous experiences of abuse. In addition to these, there are many

> **Exercise 5.6**
>
> Look back over the earlier chapters and seek out pointers which are likely to be particularly helpful in working with children or young people who have been abused. The chapters on children's needs and on communication skills should be particularly relevant. Use the space below to note the main points and, when you have the opportunity, compare your findings with those of your colleagues.

other relevant issues that we have already covered at various points within the book. These form the basis of Exercise 5.6.

We shall return to the subject of managing difficult behaviour in Chapter 7.

Dealing with children's feelings

Melzak (1992) comments that:

> From the child's point of view, the experience of physical aggression by adults can produce a variety of contradictory negative feelings eg fear, anger, helplessness, humiliation, unhappiness, worthlessness and confusion. The child can feel that she must be monstrous to deserve such frequent unpleasant treatment; she can also feel that she is the cause of her parents' distress, rage and misery (Evert and Irne 1987). (p. 102)

Experience of working with children who have been subject to other forms of abuse shows us that contradictory and predominantly negative feelings do not apply only to victims of physical abuse. One particularly common characteristic is a feeling of worthlessness, of low self-esteem. It is therefore necessary, as I have emphasised, to ensure that our dealings with children and young people reinforce self-esteem rather than undermine it.

Often, however, children need help to deal with their own feelings. They have such intense and confused feelings pent up inside them that they may need skilled help in learning how to deal with them:

> Staff require skills in exploring how the child or other person may best be enabled to express and deal with very painful feelings. Among others, feelings of guilt, shame, anger resentment, powerlessness, fear, sorrow, loss, betrayal and loss of self-esteem may be experienced. (DOH, 1991, p. 54)

To develop these skills it will be necessary for you to attend training courses, to learn from your more experienced colleagues and learn from your own experience of working with children. Despite the importance of this type of work, there can be no short cuts, although basic skills in dealing sensitively with children can be put to good use while you are building up this experience. In addition, the following pointers should help you in making progress in the right direction:

- Don't push children into talking about their feelings; they will need to go at their own pace.
- Be clear about your own feelings so that they do not act as a barrier to working effectively with the child:

> Child sexual abuse leaves us feeling de-skilled and helpless, and with a variety of emotions based on our own experiences. It is important to be clear about these emotions and frame them appropriately before working with a child. The child needs the adults to be strong, decisive and clear about their professional role. She does not need the worker to fall apart at the terrible things that have happened but to be receptive and understanding of her feelings. (Kenward, 1989, p. 30)

- Resist the temptation of ignoring the feelings dimension by concentrating on more practical matters. Being practical is an important part of helping but, if we use this as a means of keeping the child's painful feelings at arm's length, it is likely to be perceived by the child as rejection.
- Beware of criticising the perpetrator; although this person may have harmed the child, there are likely, none the less, to be feelings of love and attachment mixed in with fear and resentment; passing judgement on the perpetrator is likely to exacerbate possibly intense emotional conflicts and confusions.
- Don't fall into the trap of taking on board responsibility for the child's feelings on your own; remember that you are part of a team.

This final point is particularly important, as there is a very real danger that the powerful emotions involved in working with children who have been abused can drag you down – leaving you as a secondary victim of the abuse, rather than a strength and support for the child. It is for this reason that we need to consider the worker's own feelings and what part they have to play.

Dealing with your own feelings

First of all, it is important to acknowledge that working with abused children can be very emotionally demanding. As Kenward and Hevey (1989) put it: 'Helping children who have been severely abused and neglected is thus likely to be a long and emotionally demanding process in which the resources and patience of would-be helpers are tested to the limits' (p. 209).

A Department of Health guide on sexual abuse also recognises this and links it to the need for good supervision and effective support:

> Child sexual abuse treatment work is particularly emotionally demanding of staff. Their needs for high quality regular supervision, emotional support and consultation, during and following training should be acknowledged as a means of enabling effective treatment work, whilst minimising adverse emotional and physical effects on staff. (DOH, 1991, p. 54)

Perhaps the most important point to recognise is that there is nothing wrong or 'abnormal' about being affected by the powerful and intense feelings that we so often come across in dealing with the aftermath of abuse. We should not feel guilty or 'unprofessional' for being touched by the pain, suffering and distress we encounter in the lives of children and young people who have been abused. The difficult task we face is to maintain a balance between trying to deny our feelings (the 'stiff upper lip' approach) and allowing the feelings to paralyse us into inaction.

Adopting a 'stiff upper lip' approach is an understandable defence against the anxieties aroused by this type of work:

> Abused children often have the sort of anxiety that is contagious and makes the worker feel uncomfortable and anxious. It is easier to block off such feelings and not to have actual contact with the child, but instead to do things for the child. (Moore, 1985, p. 71)

Although this is an understandable response, it is, none the less, a potentially disastrous one as it is likely, once again, to be experienced by the child as an uncaring or rejecting response.

At the opposite extreme, allowing our feelings to get in the way of the work we are trying to do is also a potentially disastrous mistake. As Kenward (1989) puts it: 'How do you sensitise yourself without being deskilled and indecisive?' (p. 30). In other words: How can we be in touch with our own feelings without letting them dominate and possibly cloud our judgement or sap our confidence? These are issues of self-control and ones to which we shall return in Chapter 8 under the heading of 'Self-management skills'.

The atmosphere or 'ethos' in which you work can have a big influence on how feelings are handled. Unfortunately, some establishments have a 'be tough' culture which discourages discussion and expression of feelings, and acts as a barrier to creating a supportive atmosphere in which feelings can be acknowledged and dealt with. A 'macho' ethos in which it is expected that feelings will be bottled up will make it more difficult for staff

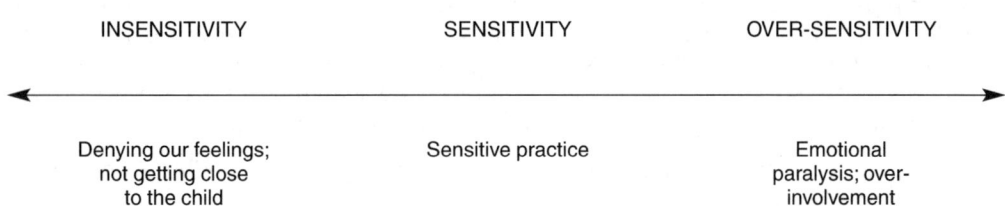

INSENSITIVITY	SENSITIVITY	OVER-SENSITIVITY
Denying our feelings; not getting close to the child	Sensitive practice	Emotional paralysis; over-involvement

Figure 5.6   Maintaining the balance

Exercise 5.7

What is the 'emotional climate' in which you work? How easy is it to discuss or express feelings? Do you help to create a supportive environment or do you find it uncomfortable to encourage the expression of feelings?

Your task in this exercise is to make sure you are clear about:

- What scope there is for dealing with feelings.
- What obstacles there are to creating or maintaining a supportive atmosphere.
- What part you can play in undermining elements of a 'be tough' culture.

You will probably find it helpful to discuss these issues with colleagues.

---

to cope with the emotional demands of the challenge of working with abused children and young people.

A note on anti-discriminatory practice

Before concluding this chapter, we need to pose the question: How does anti-discriminatory practice apply to child abuse? This is a huge question and one that we can only begin to answer here.

As far as gender is concerned, there are very clear issues in relation to child abuse, particularly but not exclusively sexual abuse. As we noted earlier, most perpetrators of sexual abuse are men, and most victims are girls. Indeed, many writers see sexual abuse as an abuse of the power of men over women (see the 'Guide to further learning' section at the end of the chapter). In dealing with cases of sexual abuse, we therefore need to be sensitive to issues of gender and take these into account in our assessment and in our subsequent work with the children and young people in our care.

Issues of race and culture are also very important. Abuse of a child can be seen as a form of personal invasion, an intrusion into one's private world, and thus a threat to identity and dignity. This is a tragedy for all children when it occurs and therefore needs to be handled sensitively. For children or young people from ethnic minorities, it is important that our practice is ethnically sensitive and not based on potentially racist assumptions or actions.

A major part of this will be to ensure, as far as possible, that black children do not have to endure racist taunts or attacks from other children.

As was emphasised in Chapter 1, the Children Act 1989 places a duty on child care workers to take account of children's racial and religious background. Ahmad (1990) summarises the situation in the following terms:

> Section 22(5)(c) of The Children Act 1989 clearly requires local authorities and voluntary organisations to give due considerations to 'the child's religious persuasion, racial origin and cultural and linguistic background': In practical terms these considerations mean ensuring proper consultation with parents and other adults who are important to the child, seeking their views, opinions and feelings, taking account of the child's views, experience and feelings in the decision making process. It also implies making appropriate arrangements for the child on the basis of due considerations given on the child's race, culture, language and religion. (pp. 89–90)

One final point in relation to child abuse and discrimination which is worthy of note is the recurring theme across both sets of issues – that of self-esteem. Sexism, racism and child abuse all have in common the tendency to undermine self-esteem and a positive self-image. This therefore underlines the crucial role of taking every opportunity to boost self-esteem and protect children and young people from the forces that threaten it.

Conclusion

Dealing with child abuse is never an easy undertaking or one that should be taken lightly. Indeed, it is a major challenge for all child care workers, particularly group care staff who may have to deal with a number of abused children at the same time.

However, despite these difficulties, we must also remember the positive aspects of this type of work:

- You provide a much needed service for children who have been let down by other important adults in their life.
- Although demanding, this type of work can also be very satisfying and rewarding.
- There are many skills to be developed gradually with training and experience – and these offer scope for continuous personal and professional development.
- Multidisciplinary work of this kind involves teamwork and therefore the pleasures and benefits of being part of a team.

Sometimes, the pressures of dealing with child abuse can lead us into forgetting the positives and thereby leaving us feeling worn down and vulnerable to stress and burnout – issues we shall discuss in Chapter 8. It is therefore important, if not essential, for you to maintain a balance to concentrate on the positives as well as the negatives. We owe it to ourselves and to the children and young people that we work with to maintain that balance.

Guide to further learning

Understanding and recognising child abuse
Beckett, C. (2003) *Child Protection: An Introduction*, London, Sage.
Corby, B. (2000) *Child Abuse: Towards A Knowledge Base*, 2nd edn, Buckingham, Open University Press.
Furniss, T. (1991) *The Multi-professional Handbook of Child Sexual Abuse*, London, Routledge.
Owen, H. and Pritchard, J. (eds) (1993) *Good Practice in Child Protection: A Manual for Professionals*, London, Jessica Kingsley.

Violence Against Children Study Group (1990) *Taking Child Abuse Seriously*, London, Unwin Hyman.

Wright, J.D. *et al.* (1991) *Frozen Awareness: A Guide to the Diagnosis and Management of Child Abuse*, 5th edn, London, HMSO.

Dealing with the aftermath

Crompton, M. (1990) *Attending to Children*, London, Edward Arnold.

Crompton, M. (1992) *Children and Counselling*, London, Edward Arnold.

Doyle, C. (1997) *Working with Abused Children*, 2nd edn, London, Macmillan.

Varma, V. P. (ed.) (1992) *The Secret Life of Vulnerable Children*, London, Routledge.

Chapter 6

Children and Young People with Disabilities

Introduction

Many staff working in group care will specialise in working with children with disabilities – for example, staff at a residential school specifically offering care and education for children with learning disabilities. However, disabled children will also feature to a certain extent in group care services not specifically for them – disability in children and young people is therefore a feature of wider child care provision and is not restricted to specialist services.

All staff working in group care therefore need to be aware of at least the basics relating to disability. It is important to understand:

i) the nature of disability;
ii) its impact on people's lives; and
iii) the implications for practice.

In relation to i), I shall show that disability is a more complex issue than most people realise. It is not simply a matter of specific medical conditions. There are also social and psychological dimensions to consider.

In relation to ii), I shall explore how disability has often far-reaching implications not only for the child or young person concerned, but also for other key people, such as parents and friends. In relation to iii), I shall outline some of the key issues staff need to consider when working with children with disabilities.

The remainder of the chapter is structured as follows: First I present a discussion of what disability is and, in doing so, challenge some common myths. I then move on to consider first physical disabilities and then learning disabilities. Next comes a discussion of some of the common pitfalls that we need to avoid, followed by a consideration of the principles of good practice. This leads to the conclusion and suggestions for further learning in this area.

Disability is a hotly contested issue, surrounded by many debates. This chapter will not resolve all the issues, but it should at least provide a sound footing from which to develop your learning.

What is disability?

Middleton (2000) defines disability in children in the following terms:

> Disability in children is a disadvantage which may be created by physical or intellectual impairment, or by ill health. The disabling condition can result from a wide range of causes, including accidental and non-accidental injury before or after birth, disease which may be hereditary, or neglect. Disability can be progressive or life threatening. (p. 94)

In some respects, this represents a traditional definition of disability, in so far as the problems are seen to arise from the physical or intellectual impairment itself. However, more recent developments in thinking around disability have tended to place more emphasis on the significance of the social context in which disability is experienced. As Middleton goes on to point out:

> The social model is an influential school of thought which holds that disablement is created as much by social attitudes and responses to children who have impairments as it is by any limitations imposed by the condition itself. (ibid.)

This represents an important departure in that it moves away from conventional views of disability which have been criticised for being too negative – that is, for locating the problems within the individual rather than within the wider social context.

An example of the social model would be a wheelchair user who has difficulty gaining access to a particular building. Is the *dis*ability due to the fact that the person concerned has a condition which requires the use of a wheelchair or the fact that the building has been constructed in such a way that it excludes wheelchair users?

Exercise 6.1

Think of a child or young person with a disability that you have worked with or who you know personally and then answer the following questions:

- What difficulties do they encounter as a result of their 'disability'?
- To what extent do these difficulties arise from the actual impairment or condition, and to what extent from people's reactions to that condition (the reactions of individuals and of society more broadly)?
- Are there any conclusions you can draw from this?

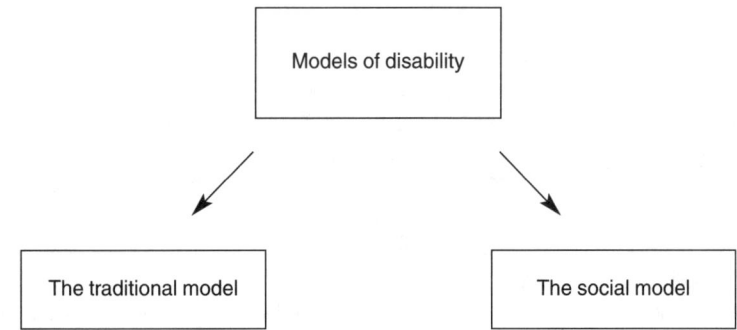

Figure 6.1   Traditional vs. social models

Disablism

The social model of disability is premised on the idea of 'disablism' – that is, discrimination on the grounds of disability. This is an important concept because what it means is that, in working with people with disabilities, we have to recognise that it is likely that they will face a degree of discrimination. This often manifests itself in terms of stereotypes. Children with disabilities are often perceived in an oversimplified way, as if they are part of a category, rather than unique individuals in their own right. For example, it is often assumed that someone who has a physical disability also has a learning disability. This can lead to disabled people being patronised.

The Children Act 1989 defines disabled children as 'children in need' (s17(10)(c)). That is, they are recognised as having a special status which means that their needs are to be carefully considered. However, regardless of any specific piece of legislation, it is important to remember that children with disabilities are *children* – we must never allow ourselves to concentrate on disability issues and lose sight of the fact that it is children and young people that we are dealing with. This is a point to which we shall return below.

Physical disability

The term, 'physical disability' is misleading in two ways. First, it tends to be used in contrast to 'learning disabilities', even though these latter disabilities also tend to have a physical basis (in relation to chromosomes, for example). Despite this confusion, the term 'physical disability' none the less tends to be used to refer to those impairments or disabling conditions which are not connected with learning or intellectual matters (the terms 'intellectual disability' and 'developmental disabilities' are sometimes used in the same sense as 'learning disabilities').

Second, as we have seen above in relation to the social model of disability, the *dis*ablement arises as much (if not more so) from the social circumstances (people's reactions, policies and systems and so on) as from the specific physical impairment. The impairment is physical, while the disability is social.

However, despite the misleading nature of the terminology, it is well accepted that physical disability relates to such conditions as spina bifida, epilepsy, cerebral palsy and so on. The actual range of such disabilities is quite vast, and so it would be hopelessly unrealistic to attempt to cover them in one small chapter. I shall therefore limit myself to a discussion of some of the more common conditions and provide some guidance (at the end of the chapter) on opportunities for further learning (books, websites and details of relevant organisations).

Spina bifida

Spina bifida is a condition in which there are problems with the transmission of 'messages' in the body to and from the brain. It is a developmental anomaly that arises in early pregnancy and affects the development of the spinal cord. It is found in three main forms, spina bifida occulta, spina bifida cystica and cranium bifida. The first of these is relatively mild and does not always have any effects, apart from occasional mobility and incontinence problems. The second causes a cyst or sac on the back, covered with a thin layer of skin and can involve a degree of paralysis and loss of sensation. In the third type, the bones in the skull do not develop properly.

Approximately eighty per cent of people with spina bifida also have hydrocephalus. This is a condition in which a build up of cerebro-spinal fluid leads to a swelling in the head which in turn tends to cause tiredness and moodiness.

Cerebral palsy

Cerebral palsy is a condition that occurs in three main forms:

- *Spastic cerebral palsy* This involves a stiffening and/or weakening of the muscles, which can affect a person's control of movement.
- *Athetoid cerebral palsy* This involves a degree of loss of control over posture and may involve making involuntary movements.

- *Ataxic cerebral palsy* This can lead to problems with balance, shaky hand movements and irregular speech.

It is caused by a failure of part of the brain to develop, as a result of complications in pregnancy or early childhood. The condition is characterised by difficulty in movement, ranging in severity from slight to considerable. Sometimes, this difficulty is accompanied by problems with sight, hearing or perception and/or learning disabilities.

Epilepsy

Epilepsy is a condition in which a disturbance in the passing of electrical signals through the nervous system leads to a seizure or 'fit'. The term 'epilepsy' is used to describe those situations where an individual has a tendency to have repeated seizures.

Seizures can range in severity and type. Some involve convulsions (jerking of the body) while others have subtler, less noticeable characteristics. How people react after they have had a seizure will vary from individual to individual, although feelings of tiredness and disorientation are not uncommon.

Sickle cell anaemia

This is a haemoglobin-related disorder. Haemoglobin is a protein found in red blood cells which carries oxygen from the lungs to all parts of the body. Normal blood cells are flexible and have little difficulty passing through blood vessels. However, where someone has sickle cell anaemia, their haemoglobin becomes sickle shaped (hence the term) and presents difficulties when it comes to passing through blood vessels. This can lead to a great deal of pain and can even damage organs in some cases.

This disorder can occur in any group of people but is mainly to be found in people whose families come from Africa, the Caribbean, the Eastern Mediterranean, the Middle East and Asia. Contrary to what many people believe, the condition is not infectious and is not a form of cancer.

These are just some of the physical disabilities that can affect children and young people, but the list is far from comprehensive. For example, we have not looked at visual or hearing impairments (see the Guide to further learning at the end of the chapter). However, what we have covered should give you enough to begin to understand the basis of some of the conditions you encounter and should be a good starting point for finding out more as and when you need to.

Exercise 6.2

Choose one of the above conditions and, using the 'Guide to further learning' at the end of the chapter, see what else you can find out about it, so that you will feel much more comfortable and better informed when dealing with a child or young person who has that condition. If you have time, repeat this exercise for one or more of the conditions.

Learning disabilities

Burke and Cigno (2000) define learning disability in the following terms:

> People with learning disabilities are those individuals who are likely to require, through actual intellectual development or delay in development, some additional support from their families, the community and a range of health, education, welfare and other services. (p. 1)

The older term, 'mental handicap', is still sometimes used by the general public, but has fallen into disuse in professional circles because of its tendency to be seen as negative and stigmatising.

One important point to note is that learning disabilities share at least one thing in common with physical disabilities, namely disablism. That is, people with learning disabilities are also likely to face discrimination. A very common aspect of this is the assumption that children with learning disabilities are necessarily aggressive, violent or dangerous to other children. As we shall see in Chapter 7, there are issues around aggression and violence that may need to be addressed in working with children with disabilities, but this is, of course, a far cry from assuming that *all* children with learning disabilities pose a threat to other children or indeed to adults. Such stereotypes are misleading, discriminatory and potentially dangerous. We should therefore be careful to make sure that we ourselves are not relying on such stereotypes and to challenge them appropriately when we encounter them in other people's attitudes or behaviour.

The most common form of learning disability is Down's syndrome. It arises as a result of an extra chromosome 21, although it is not known what process leads to this at conception. Although a relatively common condition, it is not necessarily a well-understood one. It tends to be surrounded by a wide range of myths and stereotypes. It is therefore important that we do not fall into the trap of being seduced by these (see the discussion below of pitfalls to avoid).

Waights (2003) argues that it is important to remember that:

- people with Down's syndrome tend to have poor short-term auditory memory and a shorter attention span, so it helps to break down verbal instructions into small parts and give additional time for the person to understand;
- you should be aware of all communication methods including body language, visual aids, sign language (Makaton);
- people with Down's syndrome are more likely to have sight and hearing problems and this may alter from day to day;
- receptive [language] skills tend to be better than expressive [language] skills. In other words, people with Down's syndrome tend to understand much more than they can speak. (p. 3)

Although people with Down's syndrome have a lot in common with one another as a result of the condition, we should not forget that each person is a unique individual in his or her own right. As it is often stated, we should see the person not the condition.

Another form of learning disability that is receiving increasing attention is that of autism, or to be more precise, autistic spectrum conditions. This refers to a condition or set of conditions that affect social interaction, self-awareness, the use of imagination and the use of language, amongst other things. Clements and Zarkowska (2000) make apt comment when they argue that:

> autism is not something that somebody has – a specific problem like a virus. We see it as a means of classifying people based upon the presence of certain observable characteristics. Underlying these characteristics is a wide range of differences in how the world is experienced. (p. 11)

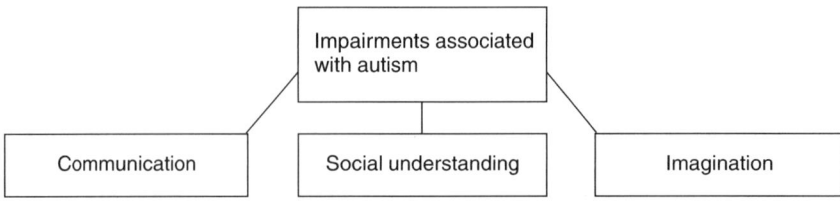

Figure 6.2   Impairments associated with autism (based on Wing, 1981)

Children with autistic spectrum conditions are likely to communicate in very restricted ways, to make little or no use of imagination, to have difficulty in 'reading' other people's reactions and in developing social relationships. Not all autistic children will display all these characteristics, but they are very commonly observed.

Working with autistic children can be very difficult and challenging for at least three reasons:

- Communication and social interaction are likely to be far more difficult than is the case with other children.
- Autistic children may present challenging behaviour for various reasons (see Chapter 7).
- There may be other difficulties as a result of, at one extreme, poor concentration and, at the other, an obsessive overconcentration on certain issues. Similarly, there may be difficulties because the child or young person lacks a sense of danger and needs constant supervision.

What is very important to realise is that working with autistic children requires a good understanding of the condition and its characteristics. For example, it would be very easy for aggressive behaviour (caused by frustration at not being able to communicate one's needs) to be interpreted as being 'naughty' or challenging a particular staff member's authority.

Other forms of learning disability that are commonly encountered are:

- *Tourette's syndrome* This is a condition of the nervous system characterised by involuntary movements and vocal 'tics'.
- *Prader Willi syndrome* This is a genetic disorder with a number of characteristics, including low stature, incomplete sexual development and a chronic feeling of hunger that can lead to overeating.
- *Asperger's syndrome* Closely linked with autism, Asperger's syndrome involves poor social communication (not being able to read body language, for example); difficulties in understanding social situations and difficulty in imagining how situations might be different.

Regardless of the specific form of learning disability, we need to remember that a feature common to all forms (albeit to different degrees) is that of vulnerability. As Burke and Cigno (2000) comment:

> A feature common to the experience of people with learning disabilities is that they are to some degree vulnerable to the influence of others throughout their lives and, depending on the severity of impairment, might only be able to lead a quality life if offered some degree of protection and support. (p. 19)

The real challenge we face, then, is being able to offer that protection and support but without being overprotective and stifling. It can be a difficult challenge at times, but it is important that we get it right.

Pitfalls to avoid

In working with children and young people with disabilities, there are very many pitfalls to avoid. Space does not permit a detailed account of these here, but I shall none the less outline a number of key problems that we should be wary of, so that we can have the benefit of learning from other people's mistakes without having to make those very mistakes ourselves. The following pointers in no way form a comprehensive or exhaustive list, but they should be enough to raise awareness of the need to tread carefully and to have our wits about us if we are not to make the same mistakes as many of the people who have gone before us in this field.

Losing the person

It is very easy to get drawn into the subtleties and complexities of particular conditions and forget that we are not dealing with *conditions*, we are dealing with *people* who have such conditions. While two people who have cerebral palsy, for example, may have a lot in common, they may actually be very different people indeed, and so it amounts to very poor professional practice to lose sight of the person. To treat them the same, because they have the same condition, is to fall into the trap of 'dehumanisation' – to forget that we are dealing with human beings; each one of us is a unique individual in our own right.

Confusing disability with inability

It is a very easy mistake to make in assuming that someone with a disability lacks the ability to do other things. That is, it is easy to overgeneralise. But, however, easy it may be, it is none the less not acceptable to fall into this trap. We must therefore be very careful not to assume, for example, that a child who is not able to shower unaided is also not capable of cleaning their own teeth. Similarly, we should be wary of assuming that a child or young person who cannot speak clearly cannot think clearly.

Being paternalistic

Many people feel sorry for children and young people with disabilities and thus feel a need to 'look after them'. This can lead to a paternalistic tendency to be overprotective – 'wrapping someone up in cotton wool', as it is often called. Certain forms of disability involve additional risks above and beyond everyday childhood risks, but such risks need to be carefully assessed so that we do not make the mistake of assuming that there are additional risks when there may not be any. Being paternalistic can undermine confidence and encourage dependency.

Overcompensating

This is similar to being paternalistic and refers to the tendency to be especially nice, friendly and helpful to children because of their disability. While there is certainly nothing wrong with being nice, friendly and helpful, it is important that we do not go overboard on this and create an unnecessarily tense atmosphere (because the children concerned feel uncomfortable about their 'special' treatment) or once again undermine confidence and encourage dependency. There is also, of course, the danger of holding back a child's development because we do things for them rather than allow them to learn for themselves. This can undermine the development of self-esteem and independence.

Exercise 6.3

Look carefully again at the pitfalls identified here and consider the following questions:

- Which one or ones are you more likely to fall into?
- That is, which one or ones are you more prone to?
- What steps can you take to guard against these?

Try to answer honestly and accept that everyone can fall into one or more of these traps, particularly at times when we are especially busy or under pressure.

Promoting good practice

Having identified a number of potential pitfalls that we should avoid, I want now to look at the other side of the coin – to establish some principles of good practice, guidelines on how to deliver high-quality care services.

Treating children as children

As mentioned earlier in this chapter, it is important to remember that disabled children are still children. For some, their pattern of development may be different from other children, but this does not alter the fact that they are going through a process of development. It is therefore important that we do not become bogged down in those needs that relate specifically to their disability and, in so doing, lose sight of their needs as children and young people.

Not losing sight of good practice in general

This is a similar point, in so far as it relates to the dangers of losing sight of the 'bigger picture'. For example, if you are used to dealing with non-disabled children and then are called upon to deal with a disabled child, you have to be careful not to see only the disability and forget about other aspects of professional good practice. For example, if there are suspicions that a child has been, or is being, abused, that needs reporting (as discussed in Chapter 5). We should be very wary of assuming that 'no-one would abuse a disabled child'. The evidence of history tells us otherwise.

Working in partnership

It certainly can be more difficult to work in partnership with some children and young people than with others, and disability can at times be a factor in this. For example, working in partnership with someone who has communication difficulties can be especially difficult. However, 'difficult' and 'impossible' are two different things. While extra efforts may be needed in certain circumstances or at certain times, this does not mean that we should give up on trying to involve children and young people in decision making.

Social role valorisation

This is a term that derives from the work of Wolfensberger (1998). Race (2000) explains it in the following terms:

> [Social role valorisation] suggests strategies to think about addressing the physical and social conditions of vulnerable people so as to increase the likelihood of their social image being perceived positively by others, and to maximise opportunities for their development of real and perceived competencies. Such strategies lead to, and are reinforced by, more valued social roles and less, or less powerful ones, counteracting the negative perceptions that feed devaluation. (p. 327)

What this means, in effect, is that it is important to work towards avoiding negative, stigmatised roles for people with disabilities and trying to create more and better positive roles – roles that are socially valued (valorised). The big question is, then: How can we play a part in helping children with disabilities take on socially valued roles?

> ### Exercise 6.4
>
> In what ways are disabled children stigmatised? What positive, socially valued roles can they be helped to play?
>
> Think about these issues for yourself but also seek out the views of your colleagues.

1	Treating children as children
2	Not losing sight of good practice in general
3	Working in partnership
4	Social role valorisation

Figure 6.3 Principles of good practice

Conclusion

Working with children and young people in group care can be demanding and challenging, as we have noted at various points. What this chapter has also shown us is that working with children with disabilities can bring additional demands and challenges. However, such work also brings additional rewards. Children and young people can face a whole range of disadvantages that can hold them back in later life (poverty, abuse, racism and so on) and some forms of disability, in some circumstances at least, can also add to this list of disadvantages. But we should not forget that a major part of disability is the *social* component, the significant role of people's reactions, for example. This means that we can play a very positive role in minimising the 'disabling' effects of society and promoting empowerment through positive role models, building confidence, developing genuine participation and partnership and, at all points, challenging negative stereotypes and unhelpful images of disability and disabled children. This is an important role for group care staff in helping to minimise the negatives and build on the positives.

Guide to further learning

In relation to the social model of disability, a very useful text is:

Oliver, M. and Sapey, B. (1999) *Social Work with Disabled People*, 2nd edn, Basingstoke, Palgrave Macmillan.

A good book relating specifically to children with disabilities is:

Middleton, L. (1999) *Disabled Children*, Oxford, Blackwell.
Also well worth reading is:
Marchant, R. (2001) 'Working with Disabled Children', in Foley *et al.,* (eds) *Children in Society: Contemporary Theory, Policy and Practice*, Basingstoke, Palgrave Macmillan.

The abuse of children with disabilities is covered in:

Westcott, H. and Cross, M. (1996) *This Far and No Further: Towards Ending the Abuse of Disabled Children*, Birmingham, Venture Press.

In relation to specific disabilities the following sources of information should be useful:

- *Autism* The National Autistic Society: www.nas.org.uk
- *Cerebral palsy* Scope: www.scope.org.uk

- *Down's syndrome* The Down Syndrome Information Network: www.down-syndrome.info; The Down's Syndrome Association: www.downs-syndrome.org.uk
- *Epilepsy* The National Society for Epilepsy: www.epilepsynse.org.uk
- *Hearing impairment* Royal National Institute for Deaf People: [www.rnid.org.uk; National Deaf Children's Society: www.ndcs.org.uk
- *Prader Willi syndrome* The Prader Willi Syndrome Association www.pwsausa.org
- *Sickle cell anaemia* Sickle Cell Society: www.sicklecellsociety.org
- *Spina bifida* Association for Spina Bifida and Hydrocephalus: www.asbah.org
- *Tourette's syndrome* www.tourettesyndrome.net
- *Visual impairment* The Royal National Institute for the Blind: www.rnib.org.uk

Burke, P. and Cigno, K. (2000) *Learning Disabilities in Children*, Oxford, Blackwell, is a useful introduction to the field of learning disability in children, as is:

Sellars, C. (2002) *Risk Assessment in People with Learning Disabilities*, Oxford, Blackwell, which focuses in particular on issues of risk.

Jessica Kingsley Publishers (www.jkp.com) produce an impressive range of books on autism and related issues (Asperger's syndrome, for example). They also publish a number of books relating to learning disability more broadly.

Social role valorisation is discussed in:

Race, D.G. (1999) *Social Role Valorization and the English Experience*, London, Whiting and Birch.

Chapter 7

Managing Challenging Behaviour

Introduction

The management of challenging behaviour can be a major undertaking in working with children and young people. Dealing with conflict and difficult behaviour is perhaps one of the greatest challenges of working in group care. It is no coincidence that it is referred to as *challenging* behaviour. It presents a challenge for all concerned.

It is a challenge in the sense that it involves balancing the needs of children with the broader health and safety requirements of both staff and children. It is a matter of making sure that aggressive, violent or other forms of challenging behaviour are managed effectively, but while also trying to ensure that no harm comes to child or staff member in the process.

It is a sad fact that, in considering the question of dealing with challenging behaviour, we have to recognise that there is a history of institutional abuse. That is, there are very many cases indeed on record of significant abuses of children and young people in group care settings. Attempts to deal with challenging behaviour which become abusive in their own right are therefore part of the history of group care. Consequently, we have to be very careful to ensure that we learn the lessons of that history and make sure that challenging behaviour is dealt with in ways that do not harm the child or young person concerned. It is vital that we learn how to help the child develop more mature ways of dealing with their feelings and frustrations, rather than allow the adults to sink to a childish level of indulging in abusive language, threats and intimidation or even actual violence. Unfortunately, there is a great deal of evidence to show that group care staff have, in the past, relied on such methods to achieve their ends – see, for example, Waterhouse (2000).

This chapter examines what is meant by challenging behaviour and considers some very common causes of such problems. This chapter also explores a number of skills that can help us to deal with conflict and challenging behaviour. Amongst such skills are those of 'assertiveness'. This involves finding the appropriate and constructive balance between being submissive and being aggressive. The benefits of finding this balance will be explained and we shall consider the steps that need to be taken to achieve such a balance. Assertiveness is, amongst other things, a useful strategy for dealing with conflict. However, we shall also explore some of the other skills involved in managing conflict. We shall look at methods that can be used to prevent conflict situations from getting out of hand once tensions start to mount.

In addition, this chapter will outline a number of strategies that can be used to defuse tension and 'de-escalate' a tricky situation in which aggression or violence is becoming increasingly likely. We shall also explore the important principles that we need to be aware of, and put into practice, if it becomes necessary to use a 'physical intervention' – that is, to restrain a child or young person physically. Working with children and young people inevitably involves a degree of conflict. Sometimes this conflict overspills into aggression or even violence which leads to the child or young person needing to be physically controlled. This book cannot teach you self-defence skills or safe physical methods of restraining children, but it can at least help you understand the principles that need to be adhered to in using such physical interventions.

Finally, the chapter explores some of the issues we need to consider in helping children and young people (and ourselves) to calm down and recover our composure after an aggressive or violent incident.

In sum, then, what this chapter offers is useful and important guidance on how to:

- develop the skills of assertiveness to help to avoid the need for aggression or violence;
- manage conflict constructively as and when it does arise;
- try to defuse aggressive situations when they occur;
- understand the principles involved in the use of 'physical interventions'; and
- help people calm down during or after a tense situation.

Children and young people in group care situations will often feel insecure, for understandable reasons. Often that insecurity will manifest itself in challenging behaviour – behaviour that can be very testing for staff. It is as if the child or young person is saying: 'If you are not strong enough to control me, you cannot be strong enough to protect me and make me feel secure, so let's see how well you cope with what I can hurl at you'. This chapter is geared towards helping you to withstand that testing, so that you can go on to play an important role in bringing security to the lives of children and young people who may have gone through some very damaging experiences.

What is challenging behaviour?

Emerson (1995) defines challenging behaviour as:

> culturally abnormal behaviour(s) of such an intensity, frequency or duration that the physical safety of the person or others is likely to be placed in serious jeopardy, or behaviour which is seriously likely to limit use of, or result in the person being denied access to ordinary community facilities. (p. 4, cited in Allen, 2002, p. 3)

It is important to remember that such behaviours can be *challenging* for all concerned:

- For the child or young person concerned – such behaviour can lead to significant unwanted consequences (breakdown of relationships, disruption of education, retaliatory violence from other children and so on).
- For other children and young people – it can be very intimidating, unsettling and distressing to be exposed to other people's challenging behaviour.
- For parents or carers – in addition to the physical risk is the emotional stress that can arise.
- For staff – it can be very daunting to face challenging behaviour, involving both physical and psychological risks (physical because of the potential for violence and psychological because of the possible emotional stresses involved).

It is clear, then, that challenging behaviour is an important topic and one that deserves careful consideration and sensitive handling.

When we begin to consider what causes challenging behaviour, we very quickly realise that this is a very big question indeed. For present purposes I will break it down into three main elements (while recognising that this is a far from comprehensive overview of this very complex topic).

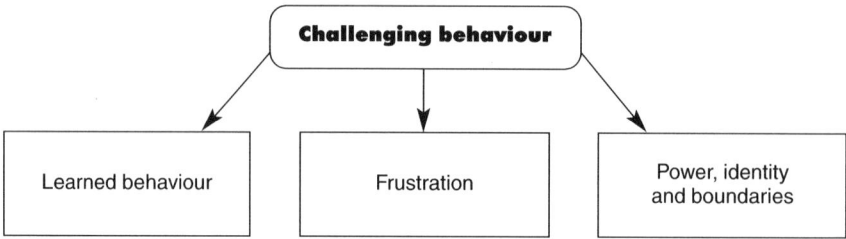

Figure 7.1 Factors contributing to challenging behaviour

Learned behaviour

It can be argued that challenging behaviour is like any other form of behaviour, in the sense that it is *learned* behaviour. According to this view, people who present challenging behaviour have learned to respond to situations in particular ways, and that these ways of behaving have a 'pay off' – that is, the child or young person is rewarded for their behaviour (by receiving attention or getting their own way, for example). They have not learned more appropriate or less problematic ways of behaving, and so rely on this very narrow set of (challenging) behaviours – what is often referred to as a 'behavioural repertoire'.

In this respect, challenging behaviour can be seen as an exaggerated form of 'normal' behaviour, in the sense that it fulfils a similar function to more common forms of behaviour.

Frustration

It can be seen that challenging behaviour has a communicative function (Sellars, 2000, p. 113). That is, it can be used as a means of expressing, amongst other things, frustration. This can apply in particular to children and young people with forms of learning disability which impair their ability to express their wishes and feelings. It is understandable that someone who is not able to convey their feelings in a conventional way may become frustrated and express those feelings through aggression or other forms of challenging behaviour.

Power, identity and boundaries

Children and young people are generally in the process of developing their sense of who they are and how they fit into the adult world – they are going through a process of identity formation (see Chapter 2). This involves learning about their personal power and its limits. From this they are able to develop their self-esteem. In some cases forms of challenging behaviour can be part of that exercising of power and development of self-esteem. What differentiates this from 'normal' (that is, appropriate or non-challenging) behaviour is that the latter generally involves recognising boundaries – knowing how far to take things and when to stop. Challenging behaviour, by contrast, can be seen to occur when the person concerned does not recognise (or chooses to disregard) those boundaries.

These three elements are not necessarily contradictory or alternative versions of reality. It is quite feasible that a particular behaviour is arising due to a combination of these three sets of issues. The task of the group care worker is not to come up with a definitive explanation of a child or young person's behaviour, but rather to draw on a wide knowledge base in order to understand the reasons for the behaviour and be able to respond to it in an informed way.

Assertiveness

Having explored what is meant by challenging behaviour, it is now time to move on and start considering how best to respond to the problem. We begin by looking at 'primary preventative strategies' – that is, ways of preventing the problem from arising in the first place. One such strategy which is very important is that of assertiveness.

Assertiveness is a way of handling situations that involve conflict between two or more people and is therefore very relevant to those situations where there is a potential for challenging behaviour to arise.

Being assertive involves achieving a balance between being submissive and being aggressive. In our day-to-day interactions with people, we will generally strive to achieve a satisfactory balance between our own interests and those of the people we interact with. However, at times of conflict, maintaining that balance can become very difficult – and this is where assertiveness has a very important part to play. Assertiveness involves developing the skills and attitude of mind necessary to negotiate the resolution (or avoidance) of conflicts in a constructive way. In short, it amounts to being fair to yourself and fair to the person or persons you are dealing with. As Rees and Graham (1991) put it: 'Assertive behaviour is behaviour which enables a person to have the best chance of obtaining their desired results while retaining self-respect and respecting others' (p. 8).

Indeed, respect is a key term in assertiveness. Respecting others means not bullying them into doing what you want them to. Respecting yourself means not allowing others to bully you into doing what they want. Assertiveness is the constructive and collaborative balance in between, as Figure 7.2 illustrates.

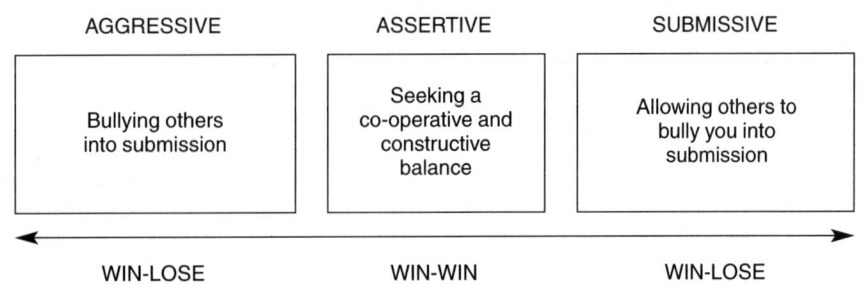

Figure 7.2   The assertive balance

Figure 7.2 also illustrates that aggressive and submissive responses to situations are, *at best*, 'win-lose' responses – that is, there will always be somebody who loses out in the situation. In fact, what is more likely is that these become 'lose-lose' situations in which both parties lose out through loss of respect for the other; tension, ill-feeling and resentment; the possibility of reprisal; or feelings of shame and regret. The assertive response, by contrast, is geared towards achieving a 'win-win' situation in which both parties achieve at least some degree of success and, in so doing, lay the foundations for future assertive interactions.

But what is an assertive response? How do we achieve assertiveness? These are difficult questions to answer but we can at least begin to answer them. Figure 7.3 gives some examples of assertive responses and Exercise 7.1 is designed to help you develop your awareness of assertiveness and your skills in achieving it. Becoming assertive is not a simple or straightforward task and takes time and practice to develop.

At this point it is as well to bear in mind that you should not write yourself off by saying 'I can't help being aggressive/submissive'. You *can* help it – it just takes time, effort and application to break old habits and develop new skills (see Chapter 8). I would therefore encourage you to persevere and not see assertiveness as something which is beyond you.

Scenario A
A young person in your care asks you to do something which you know is against the rules.

AGGRESSIVE: You shout at him or her and strongly express your disapproval.
RESULT: Resentment, ill-feeling, lower self-esteem and so on.

SUBMISSIVE: You agree to the request.
RESULT: Lack of respect for you/encouragement to manipulation; possible sanctions
                         against you by your employers and so on.

ASSERTIVE: You explain clearly why this is not possible in a firm but friendly way.
RESULT: Defusing of conflict; mutual respect and the basis for a good relationship.

Scenario B
A field social worker wishes to see you to discuss a child's progress. She arranges to come down on a particular afternoon when you are on duty, but an hour before your shift starts.

AGGRESSIVE: You 'bite her head off' by sharply telling her you don't have a cushy 9–5 job.
RESULT: Ill-feeling, mistrust and barriers to effective partnership.

SUBMISSIVE: You decide to come in an hour earlier than planned.
RESULT: Extra pressure, perhaps leaving you tired later in your shift; guilt feelings on the
                         part of the field worker when she finds out about the sacrifice you have made.

ASSERTIVE: You explain that you're not available at that time and you negotiate a mutually
                         convenient time.
RESULT: Both parties satisfied, mutual respect and the foundations laid for good
                         partnership work.

Figure 7.3   Assertive responses

Exercise 7.1

The object of this exercise is for you to begin to develop or enhance your assertiveness skills. It is in two parts. The first part is an observation exercise. Watch other people interacting (both in work and outside of work). Try to classify their responses to each other in terms of the three categories: aggressive, assertive, submissive. If you do this often enough you will develop a greater sensitivity to assertiveness. Compare notes with your colleagues on this.

The second part is where you try to put assertiveness into practice. In your day-to-day dealings with the children and young people you work with and your colleagues, try to achieve this very important balance of assertiveness. Make some notes about what helps you to be assertive and what gets in the way.

Handling conflict

Assertiveness can be very useful in preventing conflict situations from arising or for 'nipping them in the bud'. It can also be useful to prevent conflict situations, once they have arisen, from escalating and spiralling out of hand. However, assertiveness is not the only tool in our toolbox when it comes to handling situations characterised by conflict.

Recognising indicators

Very often incidences of challenging behaviour are predictable in so far as there are clear warning signals or 'indicators' present. These are often of a non-verbal nature. That is, a person's body language may be giving very clear signals that he or she is in danger of lashing out. An obvious example of this is eye contact. Fixed or excessive eye contact can be a very clear signal that aggression is likely to occur.

Exercise 7.2

What 'signals' would you associate with the risk of aggression or violence?

Compare notes with one or more colleagues.

If you currently work with children and young people, can you think of any particular ways in which individual children or young people give off signals?

Once we become aware of such indicators, we put ourselves in a much stronger position when it comes to anticipating whether or not 'trouble is brewing'. The more 'tuned in' we are to such signals, the safer we will be and the better equipped to prevent and/or deal with challenging behaviour.

Risk assessment

Risk assessment is a topic that has received a great deal of attention in recent years, especially in relation to child protection and managing challenging behaviour and health and safety matters more broadly. The basic idea behind it is that, while there is no proven, reliable scientific method which guarantees that we can identify and manage risks effectively, there are none the less steps that we can take in order to:

i)   Be clear about what risks are involved in a particular situation; and
ii)   Plan as carefully as possible how best to deal with such risk factors.

An important part of assessing risks in relation to challenging behaviour is being able to identify 'triggers'. This is a term that refers to those factors that can spark off a strong reaction. For example, one person may react strongly if someone picks up something of theirs without asking permission. For another person, the trigger may be a parent not telephoning when they had promised they would. Part of managing challenging behaviour, therefore, is getting to know the children and young people you work with and being able to identify their particular triggers.

Risk assessment is an important process, and it is essential that we see it as such – that is, both *important* (something that it is dangerous to skimp on) and a *process,* something that is ongoing. As Sellars (2002) points out, risk assessment is more than filling in a form: 'to be meaningful, risk assessment must be ongoing' (p. 11). Circumstances can change very quickly and so it is important that we do not adopt a static approach to risk assessment. The dynamic, changing nature of risk is an important idea for us to grasp.

Space does not permit a detailed discussion of risk assessment but you are advised to draw on the recommendations in the Guide to further learning section at the end of the chapter and to take advantage of any training opportunities you may be offered on this topic.

Anger management

Challenging behaviour is not always accompanied by anger, but there is none the less a strong link between challenging behaviour and anger. Developing techniques in anger management can therefore be very beneficial.

Different people get angry about different things. Anger management involves, amongst other things, identifying what makes an individual angry and thus trying to prevent a vicious circle developing in which a person becomes angry and then becomes much more easily aroused, thus leading to more anger, and so on. Anger is often associated with a person's values. For example, someone who values privacy is more likely to become angry when their privacy is invaded than someone to whom privacy is less of an issue. So, if someone is regularly becoming angry, it can be very helpful to try and work out which value (or values) of theirs are being offended. This can give significant insights into how such anger can then be managed.

Anger can also arise because of irrational beliefs. For example, someone may character-istically become angry when people are laughing because they irrationally believe that they are being laughed at. Changing someone's perspective on situations and the feelings they engender can therefore also be an important part of anger management.

As with risk assessment, this is a very big and complex topic. You are therefore advised to make use of the 'Guide to further learning' at the end of the chapter and to take advantage of any training opportunities on this topic that may become available.

Other guidelines

Of course, no-one can guarantee the absence of aggression and violence or other such forms of challenging behaviour, but there are none the less guidelines that can play a signif-icant role in reducing the chances of such problems arising. Consider the following:

- *Know your child (or young person)* This may be more easily said than done, but we can start to identify certain 'triggers' (things that are likely to provoke a strong reaction) for each of the children and young people we work with.
- *Recognise arousal* Aggression and violence can sometimes be sudden and unpre-dictable, but this is fairly rare. Usually, the first step is when a child becomes emotionally 'aroused' or agitated as, for example, when frustration starts to mount. It is therefore important that you are able to recognise arousal and 'nip the trouble in the bud', as discussed above.
- *Avoid audiences* If you need to confront a child or young person over a potentially difficult situation, avoid having an audience. The presence of others can lead to either higher tension or bravado, neither of which is helpful.
- *Listen and acknowledge* Tensions tend to rise when children feel that their feelings or views are not being listened to or acknowledged.
- *Channel aggression* If tensions are running high, consider ways of channelling aggression through, for example, sport or structured activities.
- *Try to use diversion* Similarly, if a child or young person is getting agitated over a particular issue, see if you can subtly and gently 'divert' them by getting them involved in something else – one of their favourite activities, for example.
- *Keep calm, stay in control* If you begin to lose control, you will 'fan the flames' and run the risk of aggravating and intensifying the situation. Keeping calm will have the opposite effect.
- *Don't corner a child* Literally or metaphorically, beware of backing a child or young person into a corner. Always give them the opportunity to back down without having to admit defeat or lose face.
- *Don't corner yourself* If there is a risk of violence, avoid putting yourself in a position where your escape route is blocked.
- *Use support* If you get into a conflict situation, the involvement of a colleague or other person to act as a mediator can be very effective in defusing the situation. Don't look upon accepting support as a sign of weakness or failure.

Underpinning all the advice and guidance given here is the need to create the right atmosphere in the first place. That is, if group care is taking place in a context of tension, anxiety and discomfort, we should not be surprised that some people become very unsettled and thus more prone to presenting challenging behaviours. We should therefore do everything we reasonably can to create a calm, supportive atmosphere so that we are reducing the chances of problems arising. Of course, that will not solve all the problems, but it can make a hugely positive difference.

De-escalation

Once tensions begin to rise, it is very easy for a vicious circle to develop in which the tension triggers off challenging behaviour, which in turn creates more tension, which in turn leads to more challenging behaviour, and so on. It is therefore very important that we have a few tricks up our sleeve that should help us to be able to defuse tense situations – to practise what is known as 'de-escalation'.

Verbal and non-verbal

An essential point to recognise is that de-escalation needs to be both verbal and non-verbal. It is no good making calming, reassuring noises, when our body language gives off contradictory signals. For example, if we are trying to get across the message that it is important for everyone to stay calm, then we need to give that message consistently – in the words we use, the tone of voice and so on, and the body language. If these are not consistent, then we will undermine the message we are trying to put across and may actually make the situation worse.

Acknowledging feelings

When feelings start to escalate, it can be very helpful to acknowledge those feelings. For example, if someone is starting to get angry, it is generally a good idea to make it clear that you are aware of this. Acknowledging someone's feelings has the effect of validating them, whereas, if we do not acknowledge the feelings, we may find that the feelings become magnified. If someone feels left out (for example, because it is someone else's birthday and they are getting all the attention), not acknowledging those feelings can make him or her feel even more excluded.

The point was made in Chapter 4 that reflecting feelings is an important part of effective communication. This means that we need to be prepared to acknowledge (and thus 'reflect') certain feelings at certain times if we want to avoid the escalation of tension or ill-feeling.

Physical interventions: principles of good practice

Of course, there will be times when even the best efforts at 'de-escalation' will fail and we will have a violent situation on our hands. At such times it may become necessary to use what are known as 'physical interventions' – that is, it may become necessary to physically restrain a child or young person to prevent them from hurting themselves or other people or damaging property. It is essential to stress that physical interventions should be used very sparingly and only when strictly necessary. They should also be handled very carefully and sensitively and *strictly* in line with the policy and procedures of your employers.

Exercise 7.3

Have you had sight of your employers' policy and procedures on physical interventions? If not, obtain a copy and read it carefully to make sure that you fully understand what is permissible and what is not. If there is anything you do not understand, ask your supervisor or another senior colleague to help you.

   If you have already seen this document, read it again to remind yourself of what it says.

Physically restraining someone is a dangerous undertaking. The British Institute of Learning Disabilities (BILD) refers to research which:

> shows 50% of all people with intellectual disabilities and challenging behaviour are subject to physical retraint (Emerson et al 2000) and that the inappropriate use of physical restraint increases the risk of injury to service users and care staff (Allen & Tynan 2000). (2001, p. 1)

And, of course, it is not only people with learning disabilities who will present challenging behaviours. Any child or young person may, at some time or other, need to be physically restrained.

As stated earlier, this chapter is no substitute for proper training in physical interventions. However, it can contribute positively by helping you to develop your understanding of some of the issues involved. The following eight principles of good practice in undertaking physical interventions should be seen in that light:

1. *Consider the emotional impact* Situations involving physical restraint can be emotionally very intense for both the child or young person concerned and for staff members (see the discussion of 'the calm after the storm' below).
2. *It is not an alternative to preventative strategies* As Allen (2002a) comments: 'the implementation of reactive strategies in the absence of equivalent preventative strategies is unethical and unacceptable practice' (p. 71). It is vitally important that physical interventions do not happen more often than they need to because the steps needed to avoid or de-escalate situations have not been taken.
3. *Treat people with respect* Children and young people need to be treated with respect and dignity – we should never forget that, even in a highly pressurised situation involving physical restraint.
4. *Use the minimum force necessary* Being involved in a situation that requires the use of physical force does not, of course, mean that we can use as much force as we like. Using excessive force can amount to an assault, so do make sure that, in all circumstances, you use only as much force as is strictly necessary.
5. *Do not restrict breathing* It can be dangerous to restrict someone's breathing, and so this should not be used as a means of subduing a child or young person.
6. *Do not inflict pain* In the past some people have used inflicting pain as a means of controlling challenging behaviour. Many people argue that it should not be used at all, while others regard it as something that should be used as a last resort only. To be on the safe side, it is best not to use such techniques at all.
7. *Ensure appropriate recording* Any incidents involving physical interventions must be very carefully and fully recorded.
8. *Follow proper procedures* You should make sure that you are aware of your employer's policy on physical interventions and make sure that you follow the correct procedures.

While it is to be hoped that these guidelines will be useful, it has to be remembered that situations involving physical interventions need to be handled very carefully and sensitively – it can never simply be a matter of following guidelines. Clarifying guidelines can be a useful beginning but it is only a beginning, of course.

The calm after the storm

So far we have considered how to prevent or manage situations of aggression or potential violence. However, this is not the whole story; we also need to give some thought to how we cope with the aftermath or 'pick up the pieces'. Some guidelines for this would be:

- *Be constructive* Don't *promote* guilt and negative feelings by concentrating on blame. Look for the constructive lessons that can be learned from the situation, for the child or young person and for yourself.
- *Get support* Don't bottle up your feelings. Traumatic experiences can be very stressful, so make sure you get the opportunity to talk through your feelings with someone you trust and respect.
- *Give support* Don't forget that the child or young person concerned will also need support, but it will need to be judged carefully who is the best person to offer that support and how to offer it.
- *Share your experience* Give your colleagues – and yourself – the opportunity to learn from what has happened, but beware of this turning into an 'inquest' in which blame is apportioned.
- *Don't relax too soon* Adrenaline produced during an incidence of physical restraint can stay in the bloodstream for quite some time, so be prepared in case the problem flares up again after a period of apparent calm. Allow plenty of time before assuming that the situation has returned to normal. You need to remain vigilant long after the initial incident is over.

Exercise 7.4

After an incident involving the need for a physical intervention, what steps do you think will need to be taken to ensure that you, your colleagues and, of course, the child or young person concerned are well taken care of? Compare notes with your colleagues on this.

Conclusion

It should be clear from this chapter that challenging behaviour is a highly complex, specialised subject. It is a topic that you will need to keep learning about as your experience, knowledge and skills develop over time. It is important to avoid the extremes of, on the one hand, being complacent about this difficult and demanding aspect of group care and, on the other, to become too anxious about it. Because of the difficulties and demands involved it is important that we work together to develop high standards of practice in this area.

In order to develop and maintain such standards, it is important to remember that control is something to be seen as a part of caring, and not as an alternative to it. That is, although it is often necessary to control children and young people (sometimes through the use of physical force), this should always be done in a wider context of caring and not *instead of* caring.

In order to maintain that focus on caring, we should also make sure that we do not lose sight of the importance of relationships. While an understanding of behaviour management and related topics can be of great help in dealing with challenging behaviour, it needs to be supplemented with the knowledge, skills and life experience necessary to form effective relationships that enable trust to be built up, and which put us in a strong position to influence the hearts and minds of children and young people who need our guidance and support. Good relationships are rarely enough on their own, but they are none the less a basic foundation of good practice.

Guide to further learning

Assertiveness

Pruitt, D.G. and Carnevale, P. J. (1993) *Negotiation in Social Conflict*, Buckingham, Open University Press.
Rees, S. and Graham, R. S. (1991) *Assertion Training: How to be Who You Really Are,* London, Routledge.
Thompson, N. (2002a) *People Skills,* 2nd edn, Basingstoke, Palgrave Macmillan, Chapter 5.

Behaviour management
Clements, J. and Zarkowska, E. (2000) *Behavioural Concerns and Autistic Spectrum Disorders: Explanations and Strategies for Change,* London, Jessica Kingsley Publishing.
Emerson, E., McGill, P. and Mansell, J. (eds) (1994) *Severe Learning Disabilities and Challenging Behaviours: Designing High-quality Services*, London, Chapman and Hall.

Conflict management
Briault, S. (2002) *Working it Out: A Handbook for Violence Prevention in Work with Young People*, Lyme Regis, Russell House Publishing.
Byrnes, J.D. (2002) *Before Conflict: Preventing Aggressive Behaviour,* Oxford, Scarecrow Press
Thompson, N. (2002) *People Skills*, 2nd edn, Basingstoke, Palgrave Macmillan, Chapter 16.
Wilde, J. (2002) *Anger Management in Schools: Alternatives to Student Violence*, Oxford, Scarecrow Press.

Handling aggression
Geen, R.G. (1990) *Human Aggression*, Milton Keynes, Open University Press.
Leadbetter, D. and Trewartha, R. (1996) *Handling Aggression and Violence at Work: A Training Manual*, Lyme Regis, Russell House Publishing.
More, S. (1997) *The New ABC of Handling Aggression: A Personal Guide*, Birmingham, Pepar.

Physical interventions
Allen, D. (ed.) (2002) *Ethical Approaches to Physical Interventions: Responding to Challenging Behaviour in People with Intellectual Disabilities*, Kidderminster, BILD Publications.

Self-Management Skills

Introduction

Working with children and young people is not a simple matter of following orders. It involves using initiative, making decisions and taking responsibility. These involve a range of skills – self-management skills – that can be used to enhance our efficiency and effectiveness. This chapter is devoted to examining what those skills are and providing suggestions for developing and improving them. We shall begin by looking at time management and the skills needed to make the most of the limited amount of time and energy available to us. There are a number of techniques that can be used to good effect and we shall explore some of them here with a view to giving you the opportunity to develop your learning further.

Developing effective ways of managing your time is a good way of fending off stress – a particularly valuable undertaking in such a pressurised job as group care with children and young people. In recognition of these pressures I shall devote some space to developing an understanding of stress management. In particular, I shall focus on:

- the sources of stress in child care work;
- methods of coping with the pressures you face; and
- the importance of support.

Stress can have very serious consequences, and so it is essential that steps are taken to develop the skills necessary for dealing with it.

But, before beginning our discussions of such skills, it is worth commenting on the distinction between a skill and a quality. We tend to think of qualities as fixed and enduring, like patience, for example. They are usually distinguished from skills, which are learned through training and/or experience. Qualities are generally seen as a part of one's personality, whereas skills tend not to be. However, there is a danger in maintaining this distinction too rigidly. It can easily lead us into adopting a defeatist position in which we mistakenly see certain abilities as being beyond us:

- 'I'm not an organised person'.
- 'I can't help being shy, it's my nature'.
- 'I can't help getting worked up, it's just the way I am'.

These are all examples of a defeatist attitude which hinges on the mistaken belief that we are not able to learn, as if the development of new skills were beyond us. Certainly some people do find it easier to organise their time. However, this is not to say that those who do not find it easy are not able to learn. It may take longer, it make take more effort, but it is none the less a mistake – and a serious one at that – to write off the possibility of developing new skills.

It is therefore important to begin this chapter with a positive and confident outlook. Your potential for developing new skills and improving existing ones is high – but will be all the higher for not adopting a defeatist attitude that says: 'I can't'.

Time management

Time management is perhaps a slightly misleading term, as it is as much about managing energy and motivation as it is about time itself. It is not simply a matter of dividing up a finite amount of time in the most useful way possible. It is also about optimum energy levels and motivation. For example, you may be able to complete a piece of work, say a report, within an hour if you feel keen and alert, whereas the same report may take several hours to complete if you are reluctant to do it or feel at a low ebb. This, then, raises two basic questions:

- How can I organise my time to best effect?
- How can I sustain my motivation and keep energy levels high?

Let's tackle each of these in turn.

Organising your time

In many jobs, staff have little or no control over how their time is organised. They have a rigid timetable to follow or they simply wait for instructions as to what to do next. Child care work is not like that. You do have some degree of control over the use of your time, although there are clearly a number of constraints on this. There is therefore much benefit to be had from spending a little time reviewing how you spend your working time and considering whether there are ways in which the situation can be improved. Indeed, by doing this, we are already practising one of the principles of time management – that of 'time investment'. That is, it is worth spending time in order to save time.

Exercise 8.1 is designed to help you gain an overview of how your time tends to be spent – an important first step towards gaining control of your workload and the time available to you.

Exercise 8.1

For this exercise you will need to make notes over the next ten days (ten full days – that is, not counting today) of how each day is spent, including time spent in work and outside work. Filling in the Time Management Worksheets (see end of this chapter) should help you with this. Ironically, this can be a time-consuming exercise but please do resist the temptation to skimp on this. Time spent on this exercise can be a valuable investment. Only brief details are required so don't waste time putting in more information than you need to.

At this stage, this is all you need to do, to fill in the worksheets and get an overview of the demands on your time. This, in itself, is a helpful exercise but will also form the basis of another exercise below.

Having gained an overview of how our time tends to be spent, we can now start to look for patterns and common themes – clues as to how we can best organise our time. We can start to ask some important questions:

- Am I wasting time on relatively unimportant matters while other, more important, matters have to wait? (In other words, are you setting priorities?)
- Are there 'gaps' in my day that could be put to better use? Are there any opportunities for me to save time?
- What takes up most of my time? Does it need to be so time consuming? Are there any ways I could do this work more efficiently?

● Does my work overlap with that of my colleagues? Are there any ways we could work together to save time? Would it help if we swapped certain jobs (so that people do what they are best at)?

Exercise 8.2

Look back now over your time management worksheets and start to ask yourself the type of questions above. Treat it as a puzzle, a game in which you have to find possible 'short cuts' or ways of getting more done in the time available. Like many puzzles, you may not be able to spot any immediate solutions, but if you stick at it, and perhaps ask someone else's opinion as well, you should be able to make some headway. Make notes on a separate sheet of paper.

Once you have completed this task, compare notes with your colleagues and see if you can learn any tips from each other.

These are just some of the many questions that arise when we start to examine the way we use our time. What we need to do in order to develop time management skills is to get into the habit of asking ourselves this type of question and get used to seeing time as a scarce resource, one that needs to be handled carefully and sensitively.

There are a number of other methods or techniques that can be used to help you get to grips with time management. It is recommended that you read Chapter 2 of *People Skills* (Thompson, 2002a) and make yourself familiar with the useful guidelines to be found there.

Energy and motivation

As we mentioned above, time management also involves managing our levels of energy and motivation. It leads us to ask the question: How can we ensure an optimal level of motivation? Once again there are a number of techniques available.

Exercise 8.3

Look back over your time management worksheets once again. This time, however, the focus is on motivation and energy. Bearing in mind the techniques discussed in *People Skills,* Chapter 2 (for example, making sure you take a break) reconsider your worksheets and see if you can see any way in which, with hindsight, you could have used your time more effectively.

As mentioned earlier, group care with children and young people is a demanding business and so can easily take its toll on us. We therefore need to counterbalance this by making the effort to remind ourselves of the positive aspects of working with children and young people. Focusing on the positives is a much needed source of motivation and energy. Working with children is by no means an easy option, and so taking a pride and a pleasure in your work is something to be fully encouraged. If you get into the habit of seeing only the pressures, problems and pain of your work, you run the risk of entering a vicious circle in which this negative focus demotivates you, makes your job harder, makes your job more negative, and so on (see Figure 8.1). In short, being negative breeds negativity, whereas being positive acts as a source of energy, motivation and, perhaps most importantly of all, hope.

The benefits of teamwork are also important sources of motivation. Teamwork offers excellent opportunities for tackling work tasks efficiently and effectively by working collaboratively and inspiring each other to achieve high standards of work.

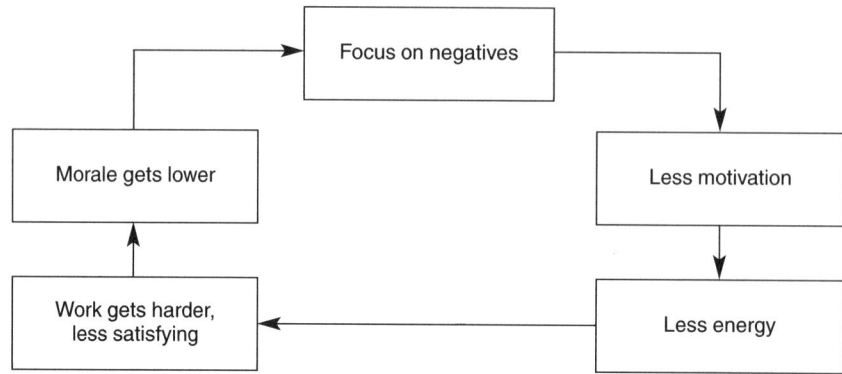

Figure 8.1   The vicious circle of negativity

Dealing with stress

Working with children and young people in a group care setting is perhaps inevitably a pressurised type of work. However, we should be careful not to confuse pressure with stress. It is useful to bear in mind the distinction drawn by Arroba and James (1987). Pressure is a 'neutral' matter, in the sense that it can be positive or negative, depending on the circumstances. Stress, by contrast, is always negative and harmful. Not all writers on the subject make this distinction, but it is none the less a useful one, and one we shall base our work on here.

In our day-to-day work, we are subject to a variety of pressures and demands. Usually, though, we are well able to cope with these. However, at times, the pressures on us can be too much and we experience the situation as stressful. We start to feel overburdened and struggling to cope. This can have a number of negative effects:

* lower morale and confidence;
* a greater risk of making mistakes; and/or
* tension and ill-feeling.

In order to understand stress, we need to consider the three sets of factors that play a part. These are:

* 'stressors': the sources of pressure;
* coping methods: the skills and strategies used to deal with the stressors;
* support systems: the network of sources of support available to us.

We shall consider each of these in turn.

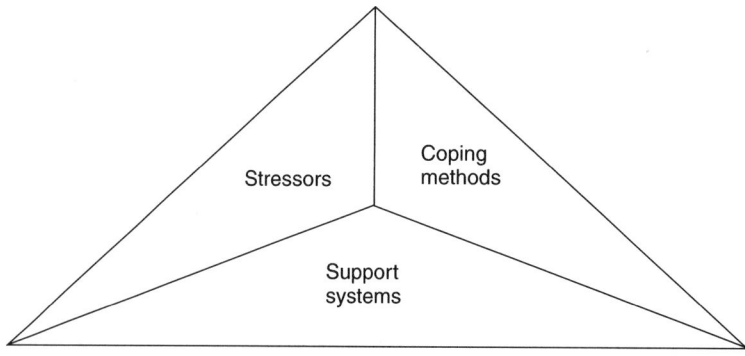

Figure 8.2   The three dimensions of stress management

Stressors

There are very many potential sources of stress in group care with children and young people. It would take a major work in its own right to cover these in adequate detail. We shall therefore have to restrict ourselves to outlining some of the major stressors likely to occur in working with children and young people in a group setting. These include:

- Dealing with loss, pain and suffering – especially with regard to children who have been abused;
- Dealing with anger, aggression and violence;
- Conflicting expectations, for example, being expected to care *and* control;
- Negative publicity and a lack of public appreciation of the difficulties involved and the successes achieved;
- Excessive or unrealistic demands made upon our time.

Of course, there are many other potential sources of stress, some that apply to all of us and others that are more personal or individual. An important part of dealing with stress is to recognise what stressors we are subject to – forewarned is forearmed.

Exercise 8.4

What stressors do you face in your work? List them on a separate sheet of paper under the headings shown below.

| Stressors that apply to child care work in general. | Stressors specific to you and your colleagues in your setting. | Stressors that apply to you particularly. |

Coping methods

As we grow up we develop a range (or 'repertoire') of coping methods, strategies for dealing with the pressures we face. In general, the more experience of life we have, the more well developed are our coping methods. Figure 8.3 shows some of the more commonly used methods.

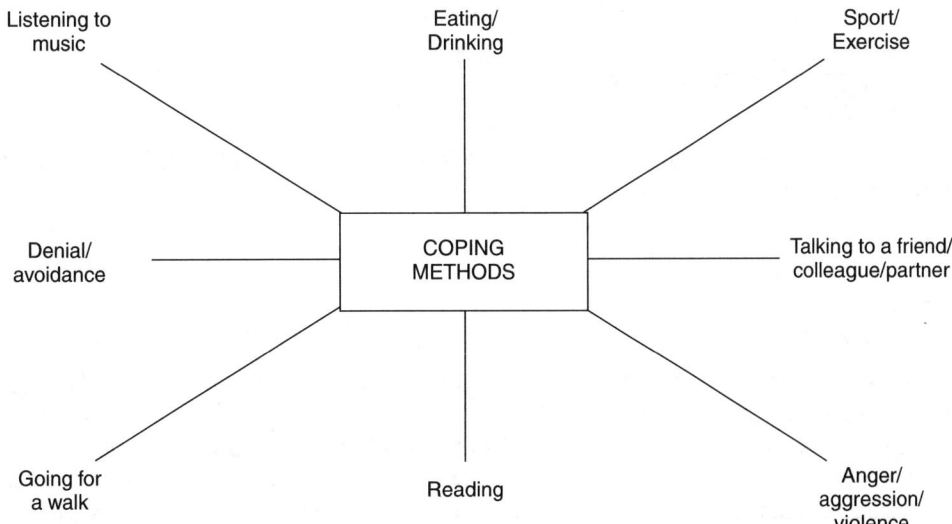

Figure 8.3   Commonly used coping methods

The methods of coping we use can be divided into two main categories: constructive and destructive. The former are those which are entirely helpful and positive, whilst the latter can be a mixed blessing, partly positive and partly negative. An example of the latter would be drinking alcohol. One or two drinks can be a useful way of coping from time to time. However, an over-reliance on alcohol can become more of a problem than the original stressor. Similarly, aggression may, at times, prove beneficial, although it is far more likely to lead to even greater problems (see the discussion of assertiveness in Chapter 7).

Effective coping is therefore based on two sets of factors:

1. Having a broad range of coping strategies – a strong repertoire – helps to prevent relying on a small number of methods. The stronger our repertoire, the greater our chance of coping successfully.
2. Reducing, or eliminating, our reliance on potentially destructive coping methods will also increase our chances of coping successfully by making us less vulnerable.

Exercise 8.5

This exercise involves three stages. First, on a separate sheet of paper list as many as possible of the coping methods you tend to use or have used. Second, underline the ones you see as potentially destructive or problematic. Third, compare notes with your colleagues and see if you can find some useful ideas for expanding your repertoire.

It is therefore important that we broaden our range of coping methods whenever possible, whilst at the same time trying to avoid using potentially destructive ways of coping with pressure.

Support systems

Support systems can also be divided into two categories: formal and informal. Formal support derives from a number of work-based sources:

- supervision;
- mentoring;
- training;
- appraisal/developmental reviews;
- and so on.

In addition to these, we have a number of informal sources of support both within, and outside of, work:

- colleagues;
- partner/family;
- friends;
- and so on.

Unfortunately, one of the main barriers to receiving support can be our own attitude, especially if this is reinforced by a macho 'be tough' culture in our workbase. What needs to change most of all if stress is to be any less of a problem is the view that needing support is a sign of weakness or inadequacy. Stress should be seen not as a failing on the part of the individual, but rather a reflection of the difficult circumstances and challenges faced by staff in group care with children and young people. As Pottage and Evans (1991) comment:

A shift from the traditional view of stress as a personal problem located in individuals, towards seeing it as the indicator of the ineffectiveness of work environments systems and practices is necessary. Using this perspective stress is a component in quality assurance. (p. 12)

Blaming ourselves for pressure and stress does not help the situation and, if anything, tends to make matters worse, leading to additional pressure and a lowering of morale. It is therefore important to get the balance right. We must recognise what part we play in the situation (how we deal with pressures, how we respond to others, and so on) but we must also see this in the wider context (the major pressures, the availability of support and so on).

Stress management

There are no simple solutions as far as dealing with stress is concerned. However, in addition to the guidance already mentioned in relation to stressors, coping and support, the following pointers should also prove helpful:

- Talk about your pressures and your feelings. Don't 'bottle them up'.
- Try to be positive and optimistic – it makes the pressures more bearable.
- Don't try to cope alone. Most of the pressures you face also affect your colleagues – tackle the pressures *together*.
- Look after yourself. Make sure you eat sensibly, get plenty of exercise and so on. Letting these things slide will undermine your coping resources.
- Don't blame yourself. Stress can make us feel guilty and responsible for the situations we face. Beware of the 'self-blame' that stress so often causes.

Conclusion

In working with children and young people, we are called upon to complete a wide range of tasks and cope with a wide range of pressures (including the management of conflict, aggression and possible violence, as discussed in Chapter 7). Self-management skills are therefore an important part of the repertoire needed to be an effective worker in group care with children and young people. This chapter has reviewed some of the key elements of this important area of skill development. However, it is important to recognise that there is much more yet to be learned. We have only begun a process which can – and should – go on throughout your career in a spirit of continuous personal and professional development (a point to which I shall return below).

I commented in the introduction to this chapter that there is a danger that some people will resist entering into this process of skill development by arguing that they cannot change. Having looked at a number of suggestions and guidelines as to how people can change, another form of resistance to learning can be identified. In discussing dealing with aggression and violence, More (1990) comments that:

There is no way that we can make ourselves totally safe. I find that many workers will resist and reject every suggestion to improve their safety because they can identify occasions when it would not give the desired protection. This is dangerous thinking, better to be 50% safe than to trust our safety to 100% luck. (p. 42)

This argument can be applied more widely to the other skill development areas. Not all of the guidance offered here will work all of the time. However, to reject it all and 'stick to common sense', as I am sure some workers will be tempted to do, is a dangerous step, and one that amounts to 'throwing out the baby with the bath water' – hardly a good strategy for child care workers!

A more constructive approach is to find the guidance that works for you and then build on the success this brings. In social care, no-one can give us 'the right answers' but, as I hope this book has shown, you can be given guidance through this complex and demanding type of work. Responding to this guidance and using it, as far as possible, to enhance your work performance, skills and job satisfaction involves, of course, another key self-management skill: that of promoting our own learning and gaining the maximum potential for development from our experience.

Guide to further learning

Self-management skills – general
Murdock, A. and Scutt, C. (1993) *Personal Effectiveness*, Oxford, ButterworthHeinemann.
Thompson, N. (2002) *People Skills*, 2ⁿᵈ edn, Basingstoke, Palgrave Macmillan, Part One.

Time management
Amos, J-A. (1998) *Managing Your Time,* Plymouth, How To Books.
Douglass, M. (1998) *ABC Time Tips*, London, McGraw-Hill.
Eisenberg, R. and Kelly, K. (1986) *Organise Yourself*, London, Piatkus.
Thompson, N. (2002) *People Skills*, 2ⁿᵈ edn, Basingstoke, Palgrave Macmillan, Chapter 2.

Stress
Arroba, K. and James, T. (1987) *Pressure at Work: A Survival Guide*, London, McGraw-Hill.
Burnard, P. (1991) *Coping with Stress in the Health Professions*, London, Chapman Hall.
Pottage, D. and Evans, M. (1992) *Workbased Stress: Prescription is Not the Cure*, London, NISW.
Thompson, N., Murphy, M. and Stradling, S. (1994) *Dealing with Stress*, Basingstoke, Macmillan – now Palgrave Macmillan.
Thompson, N., Murphy, M. and Stradling, S. (1996) *Meeting the Stress Challenge: A Training and Staff Development Manual for Social Welfare Managers, Trainers and Practitioners*, Lyme Regis, Russell House Publishing.
Thompson, N. (1999) *Stress Matters*, Birmingham, Pepar.

Time Management Worksheet 1

	Day 1	Day 2	Day 3	Day 4	Day 5	
Morning						Morning
Afternoon						Afternoon
Evening						Evening

Time Management Worksheet 2

	Day 1	Day 2	Day 3	Day 4	Day 5	
Morning						Morning
Afternoon						Afternoon
Evening						Evening

Conclusion

Congratulations on getting through the book. To have got this far has involved a lot of time, effort and energy on your part – and you deserve credit for this. You have covered a lot of ground and you have been given a lot of 'food for thought'. But I hope you have gained more than this. I hope you have found the book not just interesting and stimulating, but also – and this is perhaps the most important thing of all – *useful* to you in doing your job. One of the primary aims of learning in the workplace is to help staff do their job better, to work in a more informed and considered way. I very much hope that this book is no exception to this. I hope that you feel the knowledge base and exercises provided here have equipped you well to take on the demanding duties of a child care worker.

At the beginning of the book I introduced the 'learning cycle' and encouraged you to:

- reflect on your experiences (both your practical experiences in work and the experience of working through the book);
- link your reflections to your previous experience, knowledge and learning – conceptualise how your new knowledge fits in with your previous understanding;
- experiment with your new level of understanding – put it into practice.

Indeed, this is the basis of 'continuous professional development' – not simply that you gain extra knowledge, but that you are able to put that knowledge to good use, by relating it to practice. It is therefore important that you remember to keep this process going, to carry on learning from your experience and putting that learning to best effect by using it to develop your effectiveness as a worker.

In a job as demanding and complex as group care with children and young people, we will never reach a standard where we can say that we know all that we need to know, that we have no further learning to do. I would therefore encourage you to see completing this book as part of a process rather than the end. This process is one of continuous self-development in which we constantly look for opportunities for learning and for developing our skills.

There are many advantages to adopting such an approach to your work, including:

- it increases job satisfaction and motivation;
- it encourages, and supports, high standards of practice;
- it gives a positive message to the children and young people you work with;
- it helps to create a positive and constructive work environment in which people can learn from each other.

I hope that you can find the time and energy to keep learning and to keep developing your skills. You owe it to the children and young people that you work with and, of course, you owe it to yourself.

I would recommend that you come back to the book from time to time and 'dip' into it. It contains a considerable amount of information and you cannot be expected to have taken it all in first time round. It will therefore be worthwhile for you to go through parts, or even all, of the book for a second time when you get the chance – and even for a third or fourth time later on. It will act as a resource for you and, I hope, continue to give you opportunities for learning for quite some time yet. I wish you well in this.

References

Ahmad, B. (1990) *Black Perspectives in Social Work*, Birmingham, Venture Press.

Aldgate, J. (1988) Foreword to Bryer (1988).

Allen, D. (2001) *Training Carers in Physical Interventions: Research Towards Evidence Based Practice,* Kidderminster, BILD Publications.

Allen, D. (2002a) 'Developing Individualised Risk Management Plans', in Allen (2002b).

Allen, D. (ed.) (2002b) *Ethical Approaches to Physical Interventions,* Kidderminster, BILD Publications.

Allen, D. and Tynan, H. (2000) 'Responding to Aggressive Behaviour: The Impact of Training on Staff Knowledge and Confidence', *Mental Retardation*, 38: 97–104.

Arroba, T. and James K. (1987) *Pressure at Work, A Survival Guide*, London, McGraw Hill.

BAAF (1989) *After Abuse*, London, BAAF.

Bannister, A. (1989) 'Recognising Abuse', in Stainton Rogers *et al.* (1989).

Beckett, C. (2003) *Child Protection: An Introduction*, London, Sage.

Berry, J. (1972) *Social Work with Children*, London, RKP.

Bowlby, J. (1951) *Maternal Care and Mental Health*, Geneva, World Health Organisation.

Branthwaite, A. (1988) 'Development of Social Identity and Self-concept', in Branthwaite and Rogers (1985).

Branthwaite, A. and Rogers D. (eds) (1985) *Children Growing Up*, Milton Keynes, Open University Press.

Briault, S. (2002) *Working it Out: A Handbook for Violence Prevention in Work with Young People*, Lyme Regis, Russell House Publishing.

British Institute of Learning Disabilities (BILD) (2001) *Code of Practice for Trainers in the Use of Physical Interventions*, Kidderminster, BILD Publications.

Bryer, M. (1988) *Planning in Child Care*, London, BAAF.

Burke, P. and Cigno, K. (2000) *Learning Disabilities in Children*, Oxford, Blackwell.

Byrnes, J.D. (2002) *Before Conflict: Preventing Aggressive Behaviour,* Oxford, Scarecrow Press

Clements, J. and Zarkowska, E. (2000) *Behavioural Concerns and Autistic Spectrum Disorders: Explanations and Strategies for Change,* London, Jessica Kingsley Publishing.

Cooley, C.H. (1902) *Human Nature and the Social Order*, New York, Scribner and Sons.

Crimmens, D. and Pitts, J. (eds) (2000) *Positive Residential Practice: Learning the Lessons of the 1990s*, Lyme Regis, Russell House Publishing.

Crompton, M. (1990) *Attending to Children*, London, Edward Arnold.

Cullen, D. and Lane, M. (2003) *Child Care Law: A Summary of the Law in England and Wales*, 4th edn, London, BAAF.

Daniel, B., Wassell, S. and Gilligan, R. (1999) *Child Development for Child Care and Protection Workers*, London, Jessica Kingsley Publishers.

Davies, M. (ed.) (2000) *The Blackwell Encyclopaedia of Social Work*, Oxford, Blackwell.

Department of Health (1991) *Working with Child Sexual Abuse*, London, HMSO.

Department of Health (1999) *Working Together: A Guide to Interagency Working to Safeguard and Promote the Welfare of Children*, London, HMSO.

Donnellan, A.M., LaVigna, G.W., Negri-Shoultz, N. and Fassbinder, L.L. (1988) *Progress without Punishment: Effective Approaches for Learners with Behavior Problems*, New York, Teachers College Press.

Emerson, E. (2000) 'Treatment and Management of Challenging Behavior in Residential Settings', *Journal of Applied Research in Intellectual Disability*, 13(4).

Emerson, E., McGill, P. and Mansell, J. (eds) (1994) *Severe Learning Disabilities and Challenging Behaviours: Designing High-quality Services*, London, Chapman and Hall.

Erikson, E.H. (1977) *Childhood and Society*, London, Paladin.

Evans, D. and Kearney, J. (1996) *Working in Social Care: A Systemic Approach*, Aldershot, Arena.

Evert, K. and Irne, B. (1987) *When You're Ready A Woman's Healing from Childhood Physical and Sexual Abuse by her Mother*, Walnut Creek, CA, Launch Press.

Family Rights Group (1991) *The Children Act 1989. Working in Partnership with Families, Vol 1: Reader*, London, HMSO.

Foley, P., Roche, J. and Tucker, S. (eds) (2001) *Children in Society: Contemporary Theory, Policy and Practice*, Basingstoke, Palgrave Macmillan.

Fraser, C. and Burchell, B., with Hay, D. and Duveen, G. (eds) (2001) *Introducing Social Psychology*, Cambridge, Polity.

Frosh, S., Phoenix, A. and Pattman, R. (2003) 'The Trouble with Boys', *The Psychologist,* February.

Furniss, T. (1991) *The Multi-professional Handbook of Child Sexual Abuse*, London, Routledge.

Giddens, A. (2001) *Sociology*, 4th edn, Cambridge, Polity Press.

Glaser, D. and Frosh, S. (1988) *Child Sexual Abuse*, London, Macmillan.

Good, D. (2001) 'Language and Communication', in Fraser and Burchell (2001).

Harris, J., Allen, D., Cornick, M., Jefferson, A. and Mills, R. (1996) *Physical Interventions: A Policy Framework,* Kidderminster, BILD Publications.

Honey, P. (1988) *Face to Face Skills*, Aldershot, Gower.

Kenward, H. (1989) 'Helping Children who have been abused: Questions and Answers', in BAAF (1989).

Kenward, H. and Hevey, D. (1989), 'The Effects of Physical Abuse and Neglect', in Stainton Rogers *et al.* (1989).

Kolb, D. (1984) *Experiential Learning*, Englewood Cliffs, NJ, Prentice-Hall.

Leadbetter, D. and Trewartha, R. (1996) *Handling Aggression and Violence at Work: A Training Manual*, Lyme Regis, Russell House Publishing.

Levy, A. and Kahan, B. (1991) *The Pindown Experience and the Protection of Children*, Stafford, Staffordshire Social Services Department.

Lishman, J. (ed.) (1987) *Working with Children*, 2nd edn, London, Jessica Kingsley.

Loney, M. (1989) 'Child Abuse in a Social Context', in Stainton Rogers *et al.* (1989).

Mallinson, I. and Thomas, G. (1984) *Learning From Experience*, Surbiton, Social Care Association.

Maslow, A. (1973) *The Farther Reaches of Human Nature*, Harmondsworth, Penguin.

Melzak, S. (1992) 'The Secret Life of Children Who Have Experienced Physical Aggression and Violence', in Varma (1992).

Middleton, L. (1999) *Disabled Children*, Oxford, Blackwell.

Middleton, L. (2000) 'Disability in Children', in Davies (2000).

Moore, J. (1985) *The ABC of Child Abuse*, Aldershot, Gower.

More, W. (1990) *Aggression and Violence*, Birmingham, Pepar.

Muncie, J. (1988) *Depraved or Deprived? The Problem of Adolescence*, Unit 3 of the Open University course: D211 Social Problems and Social Welfare.

Oliver, M. and Sapey, B. (1999) *Social Work with Disabled People*, 2nd edn, Basingstoke, Palgrave Macmillan.

Petrie, P. (1989) *Communicating with Children and Adults*, London, Edward Arnold.

Philpot, T. (ed.) (1987) *The Residential Opportunity? The Wagner Report and After*, Wallington, Reed Business Publishing.

Philpot, T. (ed.) (1989) *On Second Thoughts. Reassessments of the Literature of Social Work*, Wallington, Reed Business Publishing.

Pithers, D. (1987) 'Understanding Love and Loss: Child Care and the Growth of Love, by John Bowlby (1951)', in Philpot (1987).

Pottage, D. and Evans, M. (1992) *Workbased Stress. Prescription is Not the Cure*, London, NISW.

Race, D.G. (1999) *Social Role Valorization and the English Experience*, London, Whiting and Birch.

Race, D.G. (2000) 'Social Role Valorization', in Davies (2000).

Rees, S. and Graham, R.S. (1991) *Assertion Training: How to be Who You Really Are*, London, Routledge.

Rutter, M. (1975) *Helping Troubled Children*, Harmondsworth, Penguin.

Sellars, C. (2002) *Risk Assessment in People with Learning Disabilities*, Oxford, Blackwell.

Stainton Rogers, W., Hevey, D. and Ash, E. (eds) (1989) *Child Abuse and Neglect Facing the Challenge*, London, Batsford.

Thompson, B. (1990) *Identity and Role*, Workbook 1 of the Open University course: K254 Working with Children and Young People.

Thompson N. (1991) *Crisis Intervention Revisited*, Birmingham, Pepar.

Thompson N. (1992a) *Existentialism and Social Work*, Aldershot, Avebury.

Thompson, N. (1992b) *Child Abuse. The Existential Dimension*, University of East Anglia Social Work Monographs.

Thompson, N. (2001) *Anti-Discriminatory Practice*, 3rd edn, Basingstoke, Palgrave Macmillan.

Thompson, N. (2002a) *People Skills*, 2nd edn, Basingstoke, Palgrave Macmillan.

Thompson, N. (2002b) *Building the Future: Social Work with Children, Young People and Their Families*, Lyme Regis, Russell House Publishing.

Thompson, N. (ed.) (2002c) *Loss and Grief: A Guide for Human Services Practitioners*, Basingstoke, Palgrave Macmillan.

Thompson, N. (2003a) *Promoting Equality*, 2nd edn, Basingstoke, Palgrave Macmillan.

Thompson, N. (2003b) *Communication and Language: A Handbook of Theory and Practice*, Basingstoke, Palgrave Macmillan.

Thompson, N., Osada, M. and Anderson, B. (1994) *Practice Teaching in Social Work: A Handbook*, 2nd edn, Birmingham, Pepar.

Thompson, N. and Thompson, S. (2002) *Understanding Social Care*: A Guide to the Underpinning Knowledge Requirements for the S/NVQ Awards in Care at Level 4, Lyme Regis, Russell House Publishing.

Tunnard, J. (1991) 'Setting the Scene for Partnership', in Family Rights Group (1991).

Utting, Sir W. (1991) *Children in the Public Care*, London, HMSO.

Varma, V.P. (ed.) (1992) *The Secret Life of Vulnerable Children*, London, Routledge.

Wagner Committee (1988) *Residential Care: A Positive Choice*, London, National Institute for Social Work.

Waights, S. (2003) 'When the Biggest Disability is Public Misconception', *Professional Social Work,* July.

Waterhouse, R. (2000) *Lost in Care*, London, The Stationery Office.

Watson, J. and Woolf, M. (2003) *Human Rights Act Toolkit*, London, Legal Action Group.

Webb, R. and Tossell, D. (1991) *Social Issues for Carers*, London, Edward Arnold.

Westcott, H. and Cross, M. (1996) *This Far and No Further: Towards Ending the Abuse of Disabled Children*, Birmingham, Venture Press.

White, R., Carr, P. and Lowe, N. (1990) *A Guide to the Children Act 1989*, London, Butterworth.

Wilde, J. (2002) *Anger Management in Schools: Alternatives to Student Violence*, Oxford, Scarecrow Press.

Wing, L. (1981) 'Asperger Syndrome: A Clinical Account', *Biological Medicine*, 11: 115–129.

Wright, J.D. *et al.* (1991) *Frozen Awareness. A Guide to the Diagnosis and Management of Child Abuse*, 5th edn, London, HMSO.

Useful websites

Barnardo's	www.barnardos.org.uk
Child House	www.childhouse.uio/no
Childline	www.childline.org.uk
Children's Legal Centre	www.essex.ac.uk/clc
Children's Rights Office	www.cro.org.uk
The Children's Society	www.the-childrens-society.org.uk
The Commission for Racial Equality	www.cre.org.uk
Community Care magazine	www.communitycare.co.uk
The Disability Rights Commission	www.drc.org.uk
The Equal Opportunities Commission	www.eoc.org.uk
Electronic Library for Social Care	www.elsc.org.uk
Growth House (bereavement resources)	www.growthhouse.org
Human Solutions (staff support)	www.humansolutions.org.uk
Kidscape	www.kidscape.org.uk
NCH Action for Children	www.nchafc.org.uk
NSPCC	www.nspcc.org.uk
National Children's Bureau	www.ncb.org.uk
The Who Cares Trust	www.thewhocarestrust.org.uk

Notes

1. Please also see the disability-related websites at the end of Chapter 6.
2. These site details were correct at the time of going to press but may change over time.